ENGLISH PHRASAL VERBS IN CONTEXT

THE ULTIMATE COLLECTION

PLENTY OF EXAMPLES

&

SYNONYMS

Introduction

Do you find difficulties learning phrasal verbs?

Are you fed up with going over endless lists of translated phrasal verbs without finding enough examples and uses?

Do you have challenges in understanding phrasal verbs while reading or listening?

Are you looking forward to being able to using phrasal verbs while writing or speaking?

Well, the fact is learning phrasal verbs and using them is a matter of regular and constant practice as well as getting access to large numbers of examples in different contexts.

Getting to know the meaning of a given phrasal verb can make a little difference, the point is to be able to master them and use them correctly and in an effective way.

This book provides the most common collection of phrasal verbs in use. Every phrasal verb is followed by at least 6 examples taken from natural English contexts such as newspapers, magazines, blogs, social media and so on. In addition to this, a list of synonyms is presented in order to make the reader acquainted with as many variations as possible of the given phrasal verb.

By focusing on the sentences and trying to come up with a few extra examples on your own, chances are you are undoubtedly going to build up your ability to understand and use phrasal verbs with ease.

Knowledge is Power

Table of Contents

Account for

Meaning:
1. To form part of a total.
2. To explain the reason for something or the cause of something.

Examples;

➤ High-tech companies account for 32% of the total value of the payrolls in the area.

➤ Rural Americans are often older than those in other parts of America and that may account for the slower adoption rates for internet access.

➤ With the exception of very young children (and some students with disabilities), very few students misbehave simply because they do not recognize wrongful behavior. There are many other factors that often account for misbehavior.

➤ In terms of value of the exported commodities, machinery and transport account for the largest share of about 90 per cent.

➤ On-road use accounts for the largest share of transportation energy consumption in all regions of the world.

➤ Low-income and dysfunctional families in the Weathers and Liberman study, which may account for the high dropout rate.

Similar expressions;
1. To constitute ⁃ make up ⁃ to comprise ⁃ to form ⁃ to compose ⁃ to be responsible for ⁃ to represent ⁃ to supply ⁃ to provide ⁃ to give.
2. To explain ⁃ to give an explanation ⁃ to come up with an explanation ⁃ to answer for ⁃ to give reasons for ⁃ to provide a rationale for ⁃ to show grounds for ⁃ to illuminate ⁃ to clear up.

Act up

Meaning:
1. misbehave. (people)
2. fail to function properly. (things)

Examples;

➢ My phone's battery has been acting up a lot recently. Even with new technologies, batteries still get hot, drain and have a chemical death or degradation.

➢ My old foot injury is acting up again. I'm not sleeping well. I can't exercise or golf like I used to. It's time to make an appointment with my primary care physician.

➢ As usual, the elevator was acting up, which made the trip to the eighth floor an exhausting journey. When I finally got to my apartment, it was the time to go out on the terrace and start the coals and prepare dinner.

➢ I make another trip to the river and a little something happens this time. Could it be my spastic colon acting up? I took my medicine as usual before bed. It felt like my colon was in knots. Or one big knot.

➢ The teachers would call my mom and once I got home, it was over. I got beatings like you wouldn't believe. The next day I'd go to school and act up again.

➢ If teachers got to know the parents better, they would know how to deal with kids when they're acting up.

Similar expressions;

1. To be misbehave - to do wrong - to be out of line - to make trouble - to mess around.
2. To break down - to crash - to jam - to fail - to play up - out of order - to give out.

Aim at

Meaning:

1. to point or direct a weapon or a camera at a target.
2. to hope or plan to achieve something.

Examples;

- ➤ I've read an article which indicates that the current project aims at employing massive numbers of young people.
- ➤ The hunter knelt down and took aim at his target but the rabbit had already run away and went out of sight.
- ➤ Shooting at something doesn't seem like it would be that hard. See target, aim at target, pull trigger. But unless you aim well at your target before you shoot, you're unlikely to hit it.
- ➤ Come on! Won't you grow up a little bit! Don't aim this thing at me. That's crazy.
- ➤ The new computer classes aim at empowering both of the teachers and the students to use computers properly.
- ➤ In this context, enhancement is understood as interventions which aim at an improvement of human abilities and performance. Helping someone whose capacities are below average to reach the average, and helping someone already above average to reach a higher level of functioning.

Similar expressions;
1. To direct at - to point at - to target - to take aim - to set one's sight on.
2. To look forward to - to aim for - to aim to - to devote oneself to - to work for - to aspire to - to have in view.

Allow for   -   Take into account/consideration

Meaning: to consider/include something when making a plan or calculation.

Examples;

- ➤ Make sure you leave the rope slightly loose to allow for movement in case you changed your mind and decided to unload your stuff.
- ➤ There are many points to take into account before launching the campaign. Basically, we should allow for cultural and geographical differences.
- ➤ Successful people know well and take into account that outstanding achievement involves taking endless risks.
- ➤ Remember to take into account the shallowness at the end of the pool when you dive, or else you'll hurt yourself.
- ➤ Unfortunately, many people forget to take into consideration the color of the room when choosing a carpet or a sofa.
- ➤ It's a good idea to allow for some extra time when you go back home at the peak hour.

Similar expressions;

- ➤ To make room for - to remember - to provide for - to keep in mind - to bear in mind -   make allowance for - to take count of.

Amount to   -   Rise to

Meaning:

1. to be considered or equated the same as something else.
2. to become a certain total or a particular amount.

Examples:

➢ I'm warning you in advance. Copying your essays literally from the Internet rises to cheating; and they will be turned down as a result.

➢ Beating up animals or children is an unjustifiable and outrageous act. It can amount to serious crimes.

➢ Watch your words for God's sake! Your remarks are very abusive and shameful. Obviously, they rise up to an insult.

➢ Let me just work it out. Here you go, sir! If you want to pay cash, the bill including the service amounts to $ 200.

➢ The company is expanding and we are doing a great job in business. Our profits for this month only amount to a million pounds.

➢ After the surgery, the company gave him some aid but it didn't amount to much. He had to sell some of his furniture to make ends meet as a result.

Similar expressions;

➢ To rise to - to come up to - to parallel - to rival - to be identical - to be level.
➢ To come to - to total up to - to reach to - to mount up to.

Ask for

Meaning; say to (someone) that one wants them to do or give something.

Examples;

- In his eyes you are that shining new red bike. A lot of boys will ask you for a ride on your bike, but remember to stay brand new.
- There is no way you can go to ask for money and yet those people have that money through corrupt means.
- She had specifically asked for balloons on her birthday. She was ten, for heaven's sake! She walked downstairs slowly all the while wondering why she couldn't smell the sweet fragrance of the chocolate cake she had asked her mother to bake.
- I also repeatedly asked for discernment, clarity and wisdom as I faced decisions about doctors, surgeries and treatments options.
- I know the economy isn't great, but if you are providing a lot of value to your employer, it doesn't hurt to ask for a raise.
- Even if you asked for a raise and were denied, you already avoided the worst case scenario: regret. Nothing is worse than accepting a job or a promotion and later realizing you could have had more money if you had only asked.

Similar expressions;

- To request - to demand - to appeal to - to call on - to beg - to implore - to urge - to pray - to solicit - to plead with - to seek - call for - to crave.

Ask someone out

Meaning: to go on a date.

Examples;

➤ John: "I have been waiting for a good chance to ask Gabi out for months. Do you think the time is ripe?"

➤ Charles: "I observe that she has also taken a liking to you. Come on; man! take courage and go for it."

➤ I would ask someone out if I knew everything about, was good-looking, open-minded, good-humored and shared most of my interests.

➤ It is disrespectful to ask someone out in front of others; they are likely to say "no"; for it could be awkward and embarrassing.

➤ In my opinion, asking someone out isn't as easy as it looks to be, but rather it's one of the most vulnerable experiences in life.

➤ The moment I decided to erase the past, I began to keep my eyes open for someone I might talk to, or even ask out to lunch someday.

➤ Although Mark is head over heels in love with Fiona, he is too hesitant and shy to ask her out.

Similar expressions;

➤ To take out - to make a date - to date - to ask to go out with.

Back off/ out

Meaning: move away because you are scared; stop supporting a plan.

Examples;

➢ It seems that your opponent won't back off that easy since he has got more to lose than you.

➢ Never mind the watchdog. I know it very well. It would back off and run away if you just threw a few rocks at him.

➢ The investor has no right to back out of the contract as soon as it comes into effect.

➢ What a skillful driver! Although he is only ten years old, Jason has put the car in the reverse and backed out of the garage.

➢ Critics claim that Disney regularly goes back on its word, repeatedly changing the terms of "handshake deals" and preliminary written agreements, and even attempting to back out of signed contracts if circumstances change.

➢ Night was the worst time. The intensity of what he felt was unlike anything in his life before. It had frightened him and he'd backed off, uncertain about commitment. His jaw tightened.

Similar expressions;

➢ To give up - to step out - to abandon - to withdraw - to back out - to pull out - to break off - to quit - to wind up - to terminate - to drop out - to bow out.

Back up

Meaning:

1. to support someone or something; to prove something.
2. to copy computer information.

Examples;

➢ Whenever you back up your data, rest assured that all you need to do is restore your files.

➢ Don't think that you won't pay for the stupid remarks. Your mouth won't be able to back you up.

➢ By the way, the director says that you can't deal with this situation on your own. They are going to send someone to back you up just in case.

➢ Jason had got a lot of faithful friends who backed him up and stood by him for better and for worse.

➢ It turned out that we were the only group travelling without a party to back us up.

➢ Mark has informed me that he is going to be there in person to make sure we would be taken care of well and to back us up if necessary.

Similar expressions;

1. To stand behind - to stand by - to root for - to join forces - to lend a hand - to speak up for.
2. To make a copy - to make a substitute for.

Be off

Meaning: to depart or leave.

Examples;

- Peering through the crack was an attractive middle-aged woman with short salt and pepper hair. "I am off shopping, Gustav. I should be back in two hours.
- And now I get to go on vacation! I am off to Cape Breton for a bit of R and R.
- "I am visiting so and so and don't want to make a scene," "I am on vacation," "It is only a little piece,
- Vanessa and I spent the day at my place, and I put her in a cab about 6:00 PM. She was off to her Friday night gig at the Tavern.
- Lara took off her headphones, put them in her back pack and was off to her homeroom.
- They called attendance then the bell rang. Everyone was off to the backyard in a few minutes.

Similar expressions;

- To go away - to depart - to leave - to exit - to dash.

Blow someone/something away

Meaning:

1. to impress or surprise someone very much.
2. to defeat a competitor completely.
3. when the wind takes or moves something from a location.

Examples;

➤ It was a fierce competition. Everyone was so nervous as the commentator was declaring the scores. It was great to hear that our team won the first prize - that blew us away.

➤ Our performance was far below average. Consequently, we got blown away in that match, losing 10 to 0.

➤ I was almost blown away on my way home last night because of the strong winds.

➤ Where on earth is the laundry basket? It must have been blown away during last night's gale.

➤ The Inspiration 8300 was a high quality screen. Visually, the graphic results we achieved blew us away.

➤ He's an incredibly talented actor and he blew us away and confirmed all our hopes that he was our Spector.

Similar expressions;

1. Blow one's mind - to be dumbstruck/ speechless - to be at loss of words.
2. To beat - to knock out - to outplay - to win - to make mincemeat of.
3. To blow off - to blow over - to drift - to stir.

Blow up

Meaning:

1. to fill with air.
2. to explode/ destroy something or to kill someone with a bomb.
3. become angry.
4. **break out**- when a storm or an argument starts suddenly.

Examples;

- The speeding car blew up as it hit the wall. The driver was immediately taken to hospital and miraculously survived.
- I can scarcely believe our lives are to be saved. I am slightly afraid that, anyway, the house will blow up; in that case, we will all explode together.
- Fireworks are made of gunpowder. They are set off at night as part of a festival. They get shot into the sky, blow up and make colorful sparks and loud noises.
- Blowing up a balloon can take a lot of effort - your lungs have to exert a lot of force to stretch the rubber, yet when you tie it up it stays inflated with nothing.
- Too many young technicians have lost their lives when they overinflated tires that blew up in their faces.
- While we were partaking of delicate dishes, a heavy snowstorm blew up over the city. We were two miles at least from the Shubert-Riviera.

Similar expressions;

1. To pump up - to puff up - to swell - to fill - to inflate.
2. To blast - to bomb - to burst - to dynamite - to erupt - to go off - to shatter.
3. To lose temper - to be enraged - to go crazy - to burst with anger - to rave.
4. To begin to develop - to flare up - to boil over - to emerge - to arise.

Bottle up   -   Choke/ Force / Hold back

Meaning: to hold one's feelings within. Not to express one's emotions.

Examples;

- ➢ My mum always warns us not bottle our sadness up, because it will grow worse and worse.
- ➢ Let's resolve our last night's argument. You shouldn't bottle it up.
- ➢ Poor Mary got a serious disease and has to stay at hospital for months. She's paying the price of bottling up her feelings for years.
- ➢ If things go wrong like this, take action immediately or ask for help. You don't have to hold in your resentment or frustration.
- ➢ Depression is the result of holding in pain and rage. To avoid that, try to cope with frustration before it reaches its boiling point.
- ➢ As the little poor orphan appeared, I pushed my sadness from my throat into my chest and choked back my tears.
- ➢ At the thought of her dad's loss, Mary's eyes watered and she had to choke back her tears.

Similar expressions;

- ➢ To hold in - to keep back - to play it cool - to suppress - to swallow your anger - to contain oneself - to keep inside.

Boss/Order someone around

Meaning: to give orders; to keep telling someone what to do.

Examples;

➢ Don't you notice that you're overstepping your bounds, Mike! Being the one in charge here doesn't mean that you're entitled to boss everyone around.

➢ In many children's minds, Mom and Dad are always trying to boss them around. They think or say, "Why can't they just leave me alone and leave me do what I want?"

➢ Trying to put on an authoritarian voice he said, "Are you trying to boss me around, Gilly? There is only one boss around here."

➢ Bill is getting really bossy. I feel like he is ordering me around for no specific reason.

➢ But for the record, I'm doing this as a labor of love and this is the only time you're permitted to order me around like one of your employees.

➢ You will be expected to confer with others, plan with them, cooperate with them. You will not be expected to order them around. If you do, you'll be court-martialed in no time.

Similar expressions;

➢ To bully - to dominate - to oppress - to push around - to keep under thumb - to be a back seat driver - to dictate - to throw your weight around.

Break/crack a code

Meaning: to figure out a code or a secret.

Examples;

➢ If he had been able to break the code, he would have figured out what his opponent was up to next.

➢ Although thousands of people were trying to break the code of the fried chicken recipe, none of them actually did thanks to the sophisticated security procedures.

➢ To crack the communication code, you have to understand how people think, sort, and understand the world.

➢ When I first discovered that I could crack the code, I was so excited that I could hardly stand the suspense.

➢ So many consultants, academics, and authors have tried to crack the code of Southwest's excellence to optimize their work accordingly.

➢ We count on your expertise to help us crack the code and figure out what these symbols mean.

Similar expressions;

➢ To decode - to puzzle out - to figure out - to make out - to make sense of.

Break down

Meaning:

1. (a machine) to crash; to stop operating.
2. to decompose.
3. (break something down) separate something into parts.

Examples;

➢ I have to get the central heating system serviced before the storm blows up. It has been broken down for a couple of weeks.

➢ Try to be careful when using the washing machine. If it breaks down, we can't afford a new one nor can we get it serviced.

➢ The first step is to break the chicken down then season it well. Two hours later, put it into the oven.

➢ To get outstanding results, it's significant to break big tasks into smaller, more manageable parts.

➢ Large blocks of rocks from volcanoes break down over the years to form black sand and metals.

➢ Papaya and pineapple work wonders for the human body as they contain enzymes which break down soft protein.

Similar expressions;

1. To cease to function - to fizzle out - to go wrong - to give out - to die.
2. To decay - to disintegrate - to dissolve - to spoil - to crumble..
3. To take apart - to take down - to split - to divide/to cut.

Break into (somewhere)

Meaning; enter or open (a place, vehicle ..) forcibly for the purposes of theft.

Examples;

➢ A bank vault is a secure space where money, valuables, records, and documents are stored. The prospectors would often break into the bank using a pickax and hammer.

➢ But a hacker sophisticated enough to break into a military network could conceivably penetrate a bank's security.

➢ One of them stayed in the room and began questioning me. Then, I began feeling scared. He questioned me for about an hour with questions such as, when did you break into the car; where did you hide the sunglasses.

➢ In another case, a computer hacker theft ring in Russia broke into a Citibank electronic money transfer system and tried to steal more than $10 million by making wire transfers to accounts in Finland, Russia, and Germany.

➢ Hackers were breaking into bank computers and using the system to transfer large amounts of money to their own accounts.

➢ The man explained that over the weekend, someone had broken into his office and spent the majority of the time peeling back the layers of the safe to get to the week's receipts.

Similar expressions;

➢ To burgle - to rob - to force one's way into - to burst into.

Break/ Burst into (tears/ laughter)

Meaning: to start laughing or crying abruptly.

Examples;

➢ After being told the joke, Mike would lie still for some minutes, then suddenly burst into loud laughter for several minutes without stopping.

➢ As soon as I entered, dressed in yellow from top to toe, everyone burst into laughter. That was all needed to lighten everybody's mood after the debate.

➢ I'd be doing my shopping and burst into tears. It didn't matter what I was doing, I'd just burst into tears as the incident came to mind and fear struck me.

➢ In a speech class in which we were assigned to give our autobiography; our classmate, Sarah, was telling us about her father's death in a car accident; all at once she burst into tears and ran out of the room.

➢ My heart squeezed. The children broke into tears as they saw their mum taken to hospital.

➢ Although still blushing, Mrs. Han decided to enjoy the good-natured ribbing from her friends. She knew there was no malice meant, and she ended by bursting into laughter, the loudest of them all.

Similar expressions;

➢ (Tears) : to break down - to shed tears - to cry - to weep - to sob.

➢ (Laughter): to burst out - to crack up - to break up - to laugh it up - to roar with laughter - to chuckle - to split ones sides.

Break out

Meaning; (of war, fighting, or similarly undesirable things) start suddenly.

Examples;

- There is less chance that a fight will break out and if it does it will be less intense without testosterone in the driving seat.
- The new officer steps up and starts to call the names. We are in the corridor on the north side when two inmates break out into a fight. I order the other inmates to face the wall and I take off to go break up the fight.
- Soon after arriving at my rented house the storm broke out in all its fury. I had never before witnessed such a violent storm. The thunder and lightning were fierce. The flashes of lightning and claps of deafening thunder were rolling together.
- When my brother David graduated from Exeter, the boarding school in New Hampshire my parents had sent him to when the war broke out, he came back to England, working his passage as an antiaircraft gunner on an Indian freighter.
- Islamic movements expanded significantly, especially in the 1960s and 1980s when unprecedented waves of violence broke out between the security forces and the most eminent Islamic movement, the Muslim Brotherhood.
- Americans do pay out their income taxes on or before April 15 each year. A revolt broke out with its leaders declaring that the taxation was a "direct introduction of slavery.

Similar expressions;

- To flare up - to start/begin suddenly - to erupt - to burst out - to blow up - to set in.

Break up

Meaning;

1. when a relationship ends.
2. to stop a fight.

Examples;

➢ As frustration started to boil over among the crowd, a fierce quarrel took place and the police were called to break it up.
➢ Hey! Break it up, you two, what's the deal here? I said no fighting and I meant it.
➢ Nancy's return from Colorado was the turning point of her life. She broke up with her boyfriend and left London for good on that same day.
➢ The couple broke my heart when they were forced to break up against their wills.
➢ It's no simple matter to break up with your husband. You must get hold of yourself and count to ten before taking such a critical decision.
➢ No matter what you think is going on in your relationship, sometimes a break- up comes out of the blue and hits you. As uncomfortable as it may be, you need to sit down and decide that you are going to talk to the person in question.

Similar expressions;

1. To split up - to put an end to - to divorce - to separate - a parting of the ways - to terminate.
2. To keep the peace - to pull apart - to settle.

Brimming with   -   Filled to the brim with

Meaning: to be full of something (physical or emotional).

Examples;

- ➤ Her short dark hair fell into her eyes which were brimming with fear, brimming with tears that wanted to come.
- ➤ We were so glad to see Mary brimming with excitement and joy at her birthday party.
- ➤ The obvious everyday world you view is brimming with secrets of the past and the future. All you need to do is to take good steps to work them out.
- ➤ Samantha folded her arms across her chest, her eyes were glowing and brimming with defiance.
- ➤ I was so amazed at seeing an Island in Japan filled to the brim with cats.
- ➤ It was a Saturday morning and all the summer world was bright and fresh, and brimming with life.
- ➤ How on earth can I hold the cup? It's too hot and filled to the brim.
- ➤ Prior to the interview, I was excited and buzzy, and brimming with confidence.

Similar expressions;

- ➤ To be swimming in - to be filled up - to be up to the top - to be filled to the brim - to be flowing - to be pouring out - to be full up with - to be bursting.

Bring (someone) (a)round

Meaning;

1. to make someone conscious again after being unconscious.
2. to persuade or to **talk into**.
3. to bring someone or something to a specific location.

Examples;

➤ Upon seeing her lying unconscious on the floor, I dashed into the kitchen, filled a large bucket of water and threw it on Anne's face to bring her around.

➤ She won't listen to you no matter how hard you try. Let's see if Tom can bring her round. He knows well how to deal with her.

➤ My father is so relaxed and open-minded. Unless my mother intervenes, I will be able to bring him round to my point of view.

➤ Bill was taken to a nearby hospital after the accident. It took the doctors three hours of hard work to bring him round.

➤ Make sure you bring the book round in the evening. I have to prepare for tomorrow's test. I haven't cracked a book since you borrowed it.

➤ Mary called and said that she would be delighted to join us for dinner. Would you mind if I brought her round?

Similar expressions;

1. To come round.
2. To win over - to reason with - to convince - to get around – to talk into.
3. To drive - to bring along - to pick up - to collect.

Bring down

Meaning; to reduce the level, the amount or the rate of something.

Examples;

➢ Our principal responsibility is to bring down the level of unemployment.

➢ I say he does definitely take power to bring down the price of land in Canterbury from £2 to 10s. I mean it is unfair to them for the Minister of Lands to bring down the value of this land to 10s.

➢ Before approaching a bank and trying to get any kind of small business loan, do your best to bring down the amount of money you need to borrow.

➢ It took years to sell this material, because we had to mix it with non-radioactive materials to bring down the level of radiation in this shipment.

➢ In a rough estimate, it is reported that RTI campaign contributed significantly in bringing down the levels of corruption in the country.

➢ At the time, however, there was considerable consumer concern because natural gas prices were rising though it was expected by the administration to eventually bring down the prices of fuel.

Similar expressions;

➢ To knock down - to cut down - to narrow down - to decrease - to lower - to minimize.

Bring someone up   -   Raise someone

Meaning: to take care of a child or an animal until they become adults.

Examples;

> I asked myself just what was it that this woman did? what secret or strange magic did she possess to have successfully raised her children despite the odds?
> My grandma raised us as her own, she taught us how to be good people and how to love and trust others.
> She thought about her son, and waited for him to challenge her. She'd brought him up to be a man.
> Poor Sue and Jack; they fell prey to a system of injustice that allowed others to gain advantage over them. They were brought up with parents who worked all day, and didn't have any time for them.
> Children of tender age live in these houses, they are carefully and even kindly brought up; care is bestowed on their education; they are taught to sing, to play the mandolin, to embroider, and so forth.
> As a penalty for some shameful deed on the battlefield, I shall be sent off to the country to raise hens, keep sheep, and breed children if I can do it.

Similar expressions;

> To take care of - to look after - to nurture - to breed - to educate - to develop - to provide for.

Bring about   -   Give rise to   -   Lead to

Meaning: to lead to or cause something to happen.

Examples;

➢ It's an undeniable fact that the Internet brought about revolutionary changes in our lifestyles and daily habits.
➢ Although the new policy gave rise to many complaints, they insisted on going ahead with it.
➢ The government is supposed to bring about a radical change in the health care system which proved to be a failure.
➢ The development of the city brought about a proliferation of human activities. Crafts multiplied to include a whole range of new tools, devices and facilities. We also find the introduction of utensils of all kinds, jewelry, clothing, furniture and housing.
➢ Cutting spending would initially reduce some people's income, although such cuts may lead to more output in the long run.
➢ The two most common bird groups, both of which had rows of teeth in their beak, perished leaving only a third and toothless group that gave rise to all the birds of today.

Similar expressions;

➢ To set off - to trigger - to result in - to cause - to give birth to.

Build (someone/something) up

Meaning: to become stronger, better or larger.

Examples;

- ➤ It was one of my top priorities to build her up, raise her expectations and help her think good of herself.
- ➤ It's not a child's play to build up a reputation in business. It takes years of hard work and dedication to achieve that.
- ➤ The government is building up this area. It has been changed completely since we came here last time.
- ➤ Take responsibility for building up your child's confidence in her ability to solve math problems and cope with demanding tasks.
- ➤ When a team player has realized how knowledge and skills can help build up a good record of accomplishment, motivation increases.
- ➤ She bought an electronic dictionary, but she is still looking up dozens of words in every assignment. She would like to build up her vocabulary and become a better student, but she does not know where to begin.
- ➤ Honey bees find beans an attractive source of protein suitable to build up their populations although nectar is limited.

Similar expressions;

- ➤ To grow - to increase - to charge up - to expand - to improve - to back up.

Butter someone up   -   Sweet-talk

Meaning; to be nice or flatter to someone so that they will help you.

Examples;

- ➤ You've either done something you don't want me to find out, or you're buttering me up to get money. Which is it?
- ➤ Don't go too far. I was just trying to butter you up so we can go to the movies tomorrow.
- ➤ The only reason they call you a star is they can butter you up and pay you less money; that's why you always avoid promoters.
- ➤ There's nothing to talk about, and I'm not going to give him the opportunity to sweet-talk me into believing that his going behind my back was for my own good.
- ➤ The school principal has a way with children. He sweet-talked the two boys into confession almost effortlessly.
- ➤ Even kids become hypocrites when they want you to give them a service. They have been sweet-talking me to take them to the park.

Similar expressions;

- ➤ To suck up to someone - to please - to satisfy - to praise - to kowtow - to lick someone's boots.

Buy/ pay off

Meaning; bribing someone; to give someone money to do something dishonest for you.

Examples;

➢ Don't concern yourself about anything in the world; I've bought the police officer off – we're in the clear right now.

➢ Unlike most lawyers you've faced, you couldn't buy her off. She turned you down and sent you packing.

➢ The contractor of the apartment paid off the inspectors so that they wouldn't report on the safety violations.

➢ Even though they have paid the police off to set them free for few days; they can't get away with it that easy.

➢ Rumors circulated that the chief had been bought off with a large gift of gold.

➢ People engaged in all manner of illicit behavior, while being otherwise upstanding citizens, and the police could generally be bought off.

Similar expressions;

➢ To grease someone's palm - to make a deal - to pull strings - to be on the take.

Call for

Meaning: publicly ask for something or demand for it.

Examples;

➢ The legislator called for a reliance on scientific expertise and objective standards and not on religion and traditions in making the public policy.

➢ Critics and supporters alike called for improvements in security measures and health care.

➢ The protestors marched through the streets calling for respecting human rights and freedom of expression.

➢ We have been calling for reform and equality for ages, but the administration turned a deaf ear to all our requests and appeals.

➢ This article sheds light on the concerns of foreign investors who are calling for tax cut and credit facilities.

➢ The students marched to the president's office and called for his resignation over his offensive speech.

Similar expressions;

➢ To ask for - to call upon - to request - to demand for - to want - stand up for.

Call on/ upon

Meaning: to pay a visit to (someone).

Examples;

➢ The young scholar then called upon us to congratulate and thank him for the success of his late evening's manoeuver, as he termed it.
➢ I called on them in Southern California, Utah, Colorado, etc. I was seeing the buyer regularly assuring that the catalogs had our product listed.
➢ The foreign guests will call on you next Wednesday afternoon.
➢ Why don't you call on my sister when you're in Brighton?
➢ If you leave your address, I'll pay a call on you when I'm in the area.
➢ She would call on them, and then she would spend the rest of the day shopping.
➢ Organize your friends, build a coalition of local groups, and call on your local station manager.

Similar expressions;

➢ To pay a visit to - to pay a call on - to go and see - to look in on - to visit with - to go see - to look up - to drop in on - to pop in on.

Call out

Meaning:

1. **Call out (to):** to shout to get someone's attention.
2. **Call out on:** to challenge or confront someone for something they did.

Examples;

- ➢ Although Steve's claims were true, he didn't have to make a mountain out of a molehill and call her out on it. He's making a mountain out of a molehill.
- ➢ I stood out knocking at the door till my hands got tired. Then, I tried to call out to them through the window, but to no avail.
- ➢ As soon as I saw the car in flames, I went out shouting at the top of my voice and calling out for help.
- ➢ There's no point in waiting. She is trying to hold us back - let's call her out and force her to release you – time isn't on our side.
- ➢ I have a lump in my throat so big, there's no chance I can call him out on his hypocrisy. But he must pay for his misdeeds sooner or later.
- ➢ Anna kept calling out to her, but Tee never answered or took any notice of her. She kept running and playing with the children, while pointing at the blue sky.

Similar expressions;

1. To give a holler - to shout out - to cry out - to yell.
2. To question - to confront - to protest against - to call into question.

Cancel out

Meaning: to wipe out or take away the effect of something.

Examples;

➢ You can't be productive and resenting at the same time – one cancels out the other. And bear in mind that kind words are certain to cancel the bad feelings out.

➢ We can insert a controller in series before the system is set up in order to cancel out the undesirable poles and keep only those which are suitable.

➢ Unless we update the current policy, I think the surpluses and shortages would cancel one another out.

➢ Some weird feeling made me change my mind at the last moment. I went back to the list and cancelled out my name.

➢ Eventually he suggested that, as a last resort, we could cancel out the contract with our payroll company and let him do our payroll.

➢ Our power to withhold and cancel out our meetings in states and cities that do not meet our expectations for library support is a tactic we might resort to.

Similar expressions;

➢ To abolish - to break with - to neutralize - to refute - to put down - to contradict - to terminate - to end - to get rid of - to extinguish.

Can't wait (to do something)

Meaning: to be eager, excited or impatient to do something.

Examples;

- ➢ He couldn't wait to be at home. Maybe being around his own familiar things in his own environment would hasten the healing process.
- ➢ He couldn't wait to show everyone where he started his music career. He couldn't wait to tell stories about what it was like.
- ➢ I just can't wait to see him. I've really missed him, you know. Really, really missed him. So what did he say? I mean, did he just contact you out of the blue?
- ➢ Katniss and Peeta hunt and gather in the woods, and Katniss can't help but think of Gale and how she misses him. Her mind centers on him and how she can't wait to be reunited with him.
- ➢ I call this idea' 'Myth-3': the idea that it's easy to find equity-rich people who will just give their homes away because they can't wait to get rid of it. To be fair, this stuff does happen, so it's technically not a myth.
- ➢ We miss you more than you will ever know and can't wait to hear from you about your new life at Webster. Take care of yourself my darling son, and let us hear from you as soon as you have a chance.

Similar expressions;

- ➢ To count downs the days until - to look forward to - to wait impatiently for - to long for.

Carry out

Meaning: to complete a task or activity. Bring to a conclusion; accomplish.

Examples;

- ➤ This report is not only urgent but also critical. Are you sure you can carry it out on your own? If not, please let me know right away.
- ➤ On the basis of a study carried out by the Yale university, wood is rated as easy to dry.
- ➤ The professor cancelled the session as most students failed to carry out their assignments at the appointed time.
- ➤ There is a critical operation close at hand - make sure you do what's necessary to carry out the chief's orders to the letter.
- ➤ Our chances to make appeals and retrials are very little because investigation was carried out by the head detective.
- ➤ In particular, Sally Cave contributed greatly to the research and was responsible for carrying out much of the case study research across the country.

Similar expressions;

- ➤ To be bring about - to carry through - to achieve - to perform - to conduct - to function - to execute - to manage - to take a step.

Catch on

Meaning;

1. to become popular or fashionable
2. to understand.

Examples;

➤ Sports drinks have caught on as consumers have become more health-conscious.
➤ Then I caught on to what it was the man was saying.
➤ I wonder if the game will catch on with young people?
➤ It took him a while to catch on to what we meant.
➤ Being a foreigner, he did not catch on the joke.
➤ Would you mind repeating that? I didn't quite catch on.
➤ Traditional chefs in China are hoping their local specialty - spring eggs hardboiled in boys' urine - will catch on worldwide.
➤ And if design concepts from the YCC catch on, it could mean a shakeup is in store for male-dominated design teams in nearly every industry.

Similar Expressions;

1. to boom - to come in - to trend - to grow on - to set a trend - to be in demand - to be in favor.
2. To work out - to comprehend - to deduce - to make sense of - to get the idea - appreciate - to decode - to figure out.

Catch up with/ on

Meaning:

1. to move faster to reach someone or something ahead;
2. to do something that should have been done before;
3. to talk to someone you have not seen for some time and find out what they have been doing.

Examples;

➢ Ask people what they've got planned for the weekend, and there's always the one or two who respond with, "Catching up on sleep."

➢ Poor Neil! His criminal record caught up with him in business and caused him lots of trouble.

➢ These are some papers to help you catch up on some of what you missed of your classes.

➢ Unless you have enough resources, this report will catch you up on the latest government tax changes.

➢ He walked out of his room in a hurry, through the kitchen and then down the walkway. Ryland began running to catch up with the sheep.

➢ The Internet gives you the opportunity to catch on your family news readily. With this technology, you can also access a huge variety of radio stations, and catch up on the latest news.

Similar expressions;

➢ Approach – approximate – match - make progress - make good - move forward - move in on - make up.

Charge up

Meaning: to get someone excited and enthusiastic. (to be charged up: excited or enthusiastic)

Examples;

- As an opponent, Steve never bragged about beating me. He just kept charging me up and encouraging me to try again.
- The day at the fundraiser and the encounter with Kellie had charged Mary up, given her a beam of hope again.
- Do you think that the boss will succeed in charging the employees up about working overtime?
- When the day of the contest rolled around, I shined up Robbie and made sure he was charged up.
- After hearing proposals, we were all charged up, and proud to be part of such an intelligent, creative, and young team.
- In your life, the more driven you are by something, the more will you'll have for it. Find something that will charge you up, something big and exciting to accomplish.

Similar expressions;

- To stimulate - to provoke - to prompt - to energize - to empower - to liven up - to juice up - to pump up.

Cheat on

Meaning:

1. to have a secret relationship with someone other than one's partner.
2. to cheat by not obeying the rules on something.

Examples;

- There's no point in crying over spilt milk. You've cheated on your boyfriend and there's really no turning back from there.
- I have been cheated on many times. However, it has always been easy for me to terminate my relationships with the women who cheated on me and get rid of them for good.
- A: "Jacob, you cheated on me, didn't you?"
  B: "Cheated on you? So that's why you are acting so strange – you think I cheated on you! I can't believe you would even think such a thing!"
- Large companies employ shrewd lawyers who can come up with countless tricks to masterfully cheat on paying taxes.
- I believe he cheated on my tests. He was devious even though he was a likable kid. He was, nevertheless, a sneak and I didn't trust him.
- The report illustrates that 70 % of the high school students cheated on an examination within the past year. And 36% were willing to cheat.

Similar expressions;

1. To deceive - to be unfaithful to – to fool around - to play around.
2. To trick – to fake out - to make a fool of - pull the wool over someone's eyes – to screw - to take someone for a ride - to trap - to wind up.

Check out

Meaning: to examine or get more information about something; to be certain that it is true, safe, or suitable. To look at place and see what it is like.

Examples;

- ➢ We can't take a decision unless we check out their reports and make sure that they fulfilled all our conditions
- ➢ I've been taking lots of photographs, just to check out the new camera I bought for the next vacation.
- ➢ Candi was busy fixing them something to eat but he wasn't sure how long she would be working. He wanted a chance to check out Randy's files before he had Candi with him, distracting him.
- ➢ I guess I'll eventually have to take a trip down there and check the place out. You know, before we can sell it.
- ➢ After walking around the hotel, after lunch, checking the place out, the girls went back to the room to check on Ling lee.
- ➢ They would check out the whole house to see if they could find any clues, like a broken door or window or fingerprints in other rooms.
- ➢ "Let us sit down and talk a bit. Do you think that Mark is coming to make an offer?" "I doubt it. But I will check it out and call you back as soon as I know something.

Similar expressions;

- ➢ To figure out - to slice and dice - to study - to review - to analyze - to inspect - to fact-check - to make sure - to run tests on - to see around.

Cheer up

Meaning: to start to feel happier.

Examples;

- ➤ "Cheer up, love." Her mother's voice came to her. 'Pull yourself, girl. Have a drink! For God's sake cheer up."
- ➤ Rob was always an optimist and used to lift my spirits saying; "Cheer up man, things aren't that bad."
- ➤ Jane was completely depressed after the accident. So we paid her a visit and brought her flowers to give her some solace and cheer her up.
- ➤ His wife, Susan, could not understand why he felt like a failure and tried to cheer him up by pointing out all the good things he had accomplished.
- ➤ Movies, exercising, and socializing had failed to cheer me up, but reading and writing poetry became a relief. In the lower levels of the university's Eisenhower Library, I encountered the poets who would sustain me.
- ➤ My mother, picking at the food on my tray, tried to entertain me. She tried to cheer me up by telling me about some of the other children who were very sick, and how lucky I was to be there for testing.

Similar expressions;

- ➤ To give a lift - not to let someone - something get you down - to brighten up - to improve in mood - to improve in spirits - to encourage - to enliven - to comfort.

Come/ run across

Meaning; meet or find by chance.

Examples;

- ➢ I told myself that I shouldn't be proud and to simply accept any help that came across my path.
- ➢ I had never had a good recipe for tough old birds until years later when my wife, Mary, came across this recipe for white chicken chili.
- ➢ During my research I ran across many books written in Dutch and published in Holland.
- ➢ I have come across information about genetic memory, if you are interested.
- ➢ Technically, if you come across a banana tree, this is a good indication that you've come across a water source.
- ➢ She had come across the letter in a bureau drawer containing many small packets of paper tied together.

Similar expressions;

- ➢ To meet up with someone - to come upon - to chance on - to happen on - to stumble on - to discover - to encounter.

Come (a)round

Meaning;

1. To visit someone at their house.
2. to become conscious again. (opposite; to be knocked out/ to pass out)

Examples;

- The good news was that the man who had been knocked out by the truck accident finally came round.
- That guy has nothing to do with business here, tell him not to come around here anymore or else he'll regret it.
- Bill passed out when he cut his finger while slicing onions but he came round after I threw cold water over his face.
- Mary fainted at the news of her boyfriend's departure, but soon came round and felt better.
- Zachary's only problem boils down to what folks like you keep saying about him. Why don't you come around sometime and meet him. He's the cutest kid on the block.
- Listen, I've just picked up a brand new coffee in Risborough. I've got it in the car. Why don't you come around this evening, and give it a try – bring your wife if you like.

Similar expressions;

1. To call on - to pay a visit - to pay a call on.
2. To regain consciousness - to recover - to come to - to come to life – to come to one's senses - to awake - to wake up - to revive.

Come into something

Meaning; to receive property or money by inheriting it.

Examples;

- Tom is a lucky guy. He came into a large sum of money and managed to build up himself from scratch.
- Mary came into a bit of money after her father died. However, she spent it on pleasure and amusement rather than making use of it.
- We came into a good inheritance last year. But unfortunately, the will says that we can only spend it on charities.
- It is absurd to come into an old car and not to be able to sell it or even replace it with a newer one.
- According to her father's will, Jane will come into the workshop. That's sure to cheer her up because she is in love with the place.
- My father wants me to stay beside him and has promised that I will come into this farm unless I leave the town.

Similar expressions;

- To inherit - to become a heir to - to be willed - to be bequeathed.

Come into effect - Take effect

Meaning; to become official, operative or valid.

Examples;

➢ These constitutional changes and regulations took effect while you were on vacation. No wonder you have no idea about them.

➢ The first objection is that the rules are not to come into effect until they have been laid before the parliament for a month.

➢ Without formal confirmation, the ceasefire will not come into effect.

➢ The notification from the authorities confirmed that the curfew will take effect by 7:00 p.m.

➢ I started rewiring equipment, then reprogramming it so that the upgrades would take effect. "Soon I was really good at it; I was keeping up with the other techs and proving that I could handle the added workload.

➢ There's some Motrin, and a little brown bottle of pills for muscle spasms. His mother gave him some and tried to make him as comfortable as possible, hoping the pills would take effect soon.

Similar expressions;

➢ To go through - to be **in effect** - to pass.

Come up with

Meaning: to suggest or think of an idea or plan. To devise or produce something.

Examples;

➢ After six months of hard work, the doctors were able to come up with a cure for this destructive disease.

➢ If the mechanic didn't turn up, I would be forced to come up with a better solution or else I will spend the whole night in this secluded place.

➢ Where did you come up with the idea of opening a branch? We don't have enough sources to manage that in the short run.

➢ Care Home staff came up with a novel way to help their residents relax all day long.

➢ Students were evaluated on whether they were able to come up with a testable hypothesis and follow through.

➢ We came to a most exquisite place, perfect for a picnic. Mum came up with excuse after excuse, why we should not stop and enjoy ourselves.

Similar expressions;

➢ To devise - to propose - to put forward - to present - to think up - to create - to advance - to introduce - to offer.

Cool it! - Calm down - Take it easy

Meaning: be calm. Stop acting in a violent or an excitable way.

Examples;

- ➢ We waited and waited to no avail. Every few hours I would close my eyes and take a deep breath to calm down and blow off steam.
- ➢ Calm down and take a seat Bill. Things are already going out of control and yelling is no good in these cases – it will only add fuel to the fire.
- ➢ "Stop it," I said. "What is wrong with you two? You don't ever behave like this with each other. So cool it. I'm stressed out enough without having to worry about you two."
- ➢ "Let go of me and I'll calm down." "Not a chance. Not until I get some answers. What did you plan to do with that pistol?"
- ➢ Instead of calming down and taking it easy, we may go wild in our minds and do crazy things that we would not have done before the weight loss or before we ever gained weight.
- ➢ Take it easy. We'll deal with this one step at a time. Sooner or later we'll have a paternity test done and you'll be excluded. Just cool it and we'll get this straightened out.

Similar expressions;

- ➢ Chill out - let go - lay back - let it all.

Count on   -   Bank on

Meaning: to depend on someone or trust someone to do something for you.

Examples;

➤ I wish the ground swallow me before I see my mates. The whole team was counting on me, and I let them down.

➤ Tom is sensible and experienced. You can always count on him for good business advice.

➤ I was wrong when I counted on John to pick me up from the airport. He kept me waiting for hours and didn't even answer the phone no matter how many times I called him.

➤ If you are banking on getting a payment raise to get married. Then, you're barking up the wrong tree.

➤ I wish you both luck with the future, but I never solely bank on luck. The time comes when a man has to make his own luck.

➤ The buses in this area don't have a regular timetable. You can't bank on them arriving on time.

Similar expressions;

➤ To rely on – to trust – to lean on – to ride on – to turn on - to have faith in - to have confidence in - to believe in.

Cover one's tracks   -   Gloss over

Meaning: to hide the evidence of your past or bad activities.

Examples;

➢ When he heard about the inspection, Bill spent hours shredding the files to cover his tracks in order not to leave any clue.

➢ The thieves failed to cover their tracks and were caught after the police found out their fingerprints.

➢ No one was able to find out where Tom had been hiding his notes. He was very good at covering his tracks.

➢ Steven managed to cover his tracks by throwing the gun into the river, but we were one step ahead and were tracking him all day long.

➢ They glossed over the defects, hoping that customers wouldn't notice.

➢ For too long, sports journalists glossed over football's violence.

➢ The disagreement is obvious, and it would be dishonest to gloss over it.

Similar expressions;

➢ To sweep under the rug - to conceal - to disguise - to cover up - to keep out of sight.

Cut down on

Meaning: to eat or drink less of something to improve your health or to reduce the amount of doing something.

Examples;

- ➤ After watching the documentary about the harms of sugar to human body. I'm trying to cut down on the amount of my sugar intake.
- ➤ The doctor told her to take it seriously and cut down on eating fried food to control the cholesterol.
- ➤ If you want to get to work on time. You will have to cut down on the time it takes you to get ready in the morning.
- ➤ We have been a bit wasteful during our vacation. We are almost broke right now, so let's tighten the belt and cut down on our expenses for a while.
- ➤ To lose weight and get rid of your body fats, you need to cut down on the use of your car and try to walk more instead.
- ➤ The city council announced that the improvements aimed at cutting down on traffic noise.

Similar expressions;

- ➤ To go easy on - take care of - to cut back - to reduce - to decrease - to lower - to balance - to diminish - to trim down.

Cut (someone/something) off

Meaning:

1. to stop someone by interrupting or putting the telephone down.
2. to prevent people from reaching or leaving a place, or to separate them from other people.
3. to stop providing something such as electricity or food supplies.

Examples;

➤ Having a new baby can cut a young mother off from the adult world.
➤ The attorneys refused to work out a payment schedule with Respondent for overdue payments, and insisted on full payment of all arrearages, or the health benefits for Respondent's employees would be cut off.
➤ I went mad and took it out on the phone because she cut me off in the middle of our conversation.
➤ The authorities spared no effort to provide the locals with aids, but the whole village was cut off by flooding.
➤ We've just got another warning! Unless we pay the gas bill within two days, we are bound to be cut off.
➤ Sarah feels homesick and fed up. Living abroad makes her feel cut off from her family.
➤ Don't cut me off for heaven's sake! Let me make my point firstly then say whatever you wish to say.

Similar expressions;

1. To intervene - to break in - to shout out - to jump in - to interject - to cut short.
2. To close - to exclude - to lock down - to block - to shut out.
3. To disconnect - to suspend - to close off.

Cut (something) out

Meaning;

1. to stop eating or drinking something, to improve your health.
2. **(Cut it out!)** to tell someone to stop doing something annoying.

Examples;

➤ The doctor warned me against fats and stressed that I had to cut out red meat from my diet.

➤ And while you may not be sold on completely taking oils out of your diet, if you're really trying to lose weight, cutting out oils can make a big difference.

➤ Another way to save on your food budget is to cut out junk food and fast food. While stopping at a fast food chain can prove to be a time saver, it is not a money saver. Fast food and junk food are more expensive than food prepared at home.

➤ There was an abundance of noise coming from their room. You better cut it out right now.

➤ But once more—" "I thought this was going to be a civilized talk," Ricky said. Her voice quavering, Jenny said "Now you two stop. Cut it out. I've had enough." "Enough of him".

➤ He stood up, as if to say, 'Enough is enough. You have made your point. You all scare us enough. Now cut it out and allow us to get on with our game.

Similar expressions;

1. To cease - to refrain – to terminate - to abandon - to relinquish – to discontinue – to break off - to knock off - to hold - to lay off.
2. Drop it - Knock it off - Stop it – Give it a rest.

Deal with

Meaning;

1. to take action in order to solve a problem.
2. To sell or buy goods or services to and from someone.

Examples;

➢ All our sales assistants are trained well to deal with customer complaints in a friendly manner.

➢ Some say that it takes a lot of experience and courage to deal with a complex situation. But I think necessity is the mother of invention.

➢ If we are seriously willing to deal with industrial pollution and climate change, we can figure out countless techniques and tactics in no time. But unfortunately, we are all talk in this respect.

➢ There is a general belief that before the Japanese establish their factories overseas they prepare well to deal with the natives and the local culture.

➢ Symptoms of not being able to deal with stress include lack of focus and the inability to make decisions. It can decrease your ability to tolerate things other people do and prevent you from getting needed rest.

➢ Succeeding in business has always been tough. Focusing on the personal and interpersonal skills is crucial to success - particularly figuring out some cutting-edge strategies on how to deal with difficult people.

Similar expressions;

1. to handle - to manage - to take care of - to cope with - to treat - to solve.
2. to do business with - to trade - to deal in.

Do something up

Meaning:

1. to fasten something.
2. to repair or decorate a building so that it looks attractive.

Examples;

➢ Can you show me this skirt, please? Does it do up at the side or at the back?
➢ I have to dress Jenny every morning because she is too young to do up the buttons herself.
➢ Do you think we have enough tapes to do up all these presents?
➢ Our teacher used to help the boys who couldn't do up the snaps of their jackets.
➢ I called my sister to help me do the house up before the party.
➢ It took us three weeks to do up the new flat before we could move in.
➢ It's a lovely office, but it needs to be done up a bit more.

Similar examples;

1. to tie up - to lace - to zip up - to knot in - wrap up.
2. to renovate - to modernize - to restore - to refit - to smarten up - to brighten up - to fix up - to vamp up.

Do without

Meaning; to manage without.

Examples;

> I'm back simply because I couldn't do without you like the stars couldn't do without the night.
> We don't mind working anywhere, but we cannot do without tea and tobacco.
> In order to be able to do without a director, one must have been habitually and for a long time under direction.
> A man who has been long accustomed to injuring people, must have been long accustomed to doing without their love, and enduring their aversion.
> As an artist, David always says that he can't do without a studio.
> How can Mary go away without her children? As far as I know she can't do without them for a minute.

Similar expressions;

> To give up - to refrain from - to abstain from - to renounce - to give a miss.

Dressed to kill - Dressed up

Meaning; to dress stylishly.

Examples;

➢ They were ready, dressed up, like models in a fashion competition.
➢ She's dressed to kill. And, laid out with expensive clothes and jewelry. Her makeup looks like she was prepared by one of Hollywood's finest makeup artists.
➢ As Willie Smith understood it, the "guys that dressed up always got the good jobs."
➢ Shannon got there around seven thirty dressed to kill, in high spirits and brimming with vim and vigor.
➢ The Archangel was dressed to kill in an impressive suit and new shoes.
➢ We graduate more than 3,000 students every fall and spring, all dressed to kill in their ridiculous caps and gowns.

Similar examples;

➢ To dress to impress - to be dressed to a T - to be dressed to the nines - to be in high feather - to be smart - to be stylish - to be looking sharp - to be elegant - to be formal - to be fashionable.

Drop off

Meaning:

1. take someone or something to a place.
2. to start to sleep.
3. If the amount, number, or quality drops off, it becomes less.

Examples;

- ➤ Don't worry about your journey to the station tomorrow morning, I can drop off you there on my way to work.
- ➤ Sorry for being late. I had to dropped off the kids at school because the school bus was out of order.
- ➤ Can you drop me off somewhere in town? I need to do some shopping.
- ➤ I sat in the warm room for few minutes, and then I dropped off to sleep.
- ➤ Jane went back home wiped out and dropped off in front of the TV.
- ➤ After I had a big dinner, I dropped off with no trouble at all.
- ➤ The demand for mobile phones shows no signs of dropping off in the short run.
- ➤ The business had to close after the sales dropped off dramatically.

Similar expressions

1. to drive - to give a lift - to take - to carry.
2. to drift off - to take a nap - to flake out - to get off to sleep.
3. to grow smaller- to diminish - to contract - to sink - to wane - to shrink.

Drop out (of something)

Meaning: to stop being a member of something; to stop attending or doing an activity.

Examples;

➢ He is a self-made millionaire though he dropped out of school at 14.

➢ Although it has been thought that girls drop out of school because they are pregnant, recent studies show that many girls who became mothers dropped out before pregnancy.

➢ Initially, I'm working part-time so that I won't have to drop out of university. But if things got worse, I might change my mind.

➢ The science program was too hard and challenging. Consequently, most of the students chose to drop out.

➢ Nancy dropped out of the club because she had to look after her sick mother.

➢ I didn't prepare myself well enough, so I chose to drop out of the race.

Similar expressions;

➢ To abandon - to back out - to give up - to withdraw - to leave - to cut loose.

Dying to do/ for (doing) something

Meaning: to very much want to have, eat, drink, or do something.

Examples;

➢ It was a hot afternoon when we entered the camp and I was dying for a drink.

➢ I was dying to get the extended version of the news from Paris.

➢ Sit down and tell me what took place from the get-go. I'm dying to hear all about it.

➢ She was dying to meet the designers and stylists whose imaginations gave birth to the creations of the characters she wore.

➢ At the end of the twelve hours, they were dying to get out of their space-suits, have a hot shower and get to bed.

➢ We knew you were there. And that you were dying to help.

Similar expressions;

➢ To be impatient to do - to be in need of - to dream of - to crave - to lust after - to yearn for - to fancy - to ache for - to crave - to be thirsty - to be eager.

Ease off

Meaning:

1. To gradually stop or become less.
2. To give something less effort or energy.

Examples;

➤ If the rain eases off a bit after midnight, we'll be able set off early in the morning.
➤ Take your medicine and the pain will ease off in a half an hour.
➤ Mary is such a workaholic. If she doesn't ease off, she is bound to burn herself out and damage her health.
➤ As he saw the village where he was born, Jim eased off the gas pedal and the car slowed down.
➤ According to the weather forecast, the winds are expected to ease off in a couple of hours.
➤ Never mind, I will ease off pushing when I reach one hundred.
➤ No wonder your car wheels wear out in a few months. You ought to ease off the constant use of brakes.

Similar expressions;

1. To ease up – to decrease – to fade out – to wane – to drop – to diminish - to smooth over.
2. To let go – to let out – to cool out – to tone down - to lessen – to hang loose - take a break - take it easy - calm down - slow down.

(go) Easy on someone/something

Meaning:

1. To treat someone in a gentle way.
2. To not eat or use too much of something.

Examples;

➢ Go easy on Steve when you train him - he's still too young.
➢ The anticorruption campaign was loosened and the government went easy on corrupt behaviors among officials.
➢ The executive went easy on her staff during the night shift and offered to drive them home.
➢ Hey, go easy on the chocolate – there's not much left.
➢ Go easy on Bill. He's so touchy and he's also my close friend.
➢ Please go easy on the pepper. I don't like it much.
➢ Try to go easy on the pie. You know what the doctor said about your cholesterol.
➢ When a bad shot happens, which it will – accept it, move on, and try to enjoy the next one. Go easy on yourself.

Similar expressions;

1. To conserve – to cut back - to cut down on - to spare - to economize – to use sparingly - to skimp on .
2. To let off the hook – to let off easy – to excuse - to foster - to go along with - to take care of - to let go of.

Easy to come by

Meaning: easy to find or to buy. Easily available or found.
- ✓ **Opposite**: Hard to come by.

Examples;

➤ Where on earth should I find a Roman map? Do you think that such a map is easy to come by?

➤ You can ship the goods by pickups because lorries are hard to come by in this area.

➤ This is the largest market in the city. Phones are easy to come by here, I suppose.

➤ Valuable books aren't easy to come by. Most of them were wiped out during fierce wars.

➤ A well-paid job and a considerate boss are hard to come by.

➤ Gas was hard to come by. There was a time when you couldn't buy a drop.

➤ In a world where chaos and confusion is the norm and has become status quo, inspiration is pretty hard to come by.

Similar expressions;

➤ (easy to come by): no bother - no trouble - no hardship - effortless.

➤ (hard to come by): rare – scarce - sought-after like gold dust.

Eat out

Meaning; to eat in a restaurant.

Examples;

➢ I'm not implying anything about your cooking, but seriously can we eat out tonight?

➢ Although I asked Bill not to eat out during his wife's absence, he insisted on doing that. What a stubborn man! I guess he doesn't like to be indebted.

➢ Because we were busy preparing for the event, I suggested that we all ate out – my treat.

➢ Only 2 per cent of respondents said that they were alone on the last occasion they ate out.

➢ It turned out that Mum was right to hate eating out because of the cost and the hygiene issues.

➢ But I've become fed up with eating out. I've had too many disappointing meals and paid too much money for them.

Similar expressions;

➢ To dine out.

Eat up

Meaning: to use a large part of something valuable, such as money or time.

Examples;

➢ With the rapid increase the population, it is no wonder that cities are eating up more and more farmland.

➢ There's a lesson, too, he said recently, off and on, that inefficient equipment eat up the profits.

➢ Very few are heroin or LSD or the other drugs that are out there now, because it's the poor man's drug. It's got our jail overcrowded, which eats up our food budget. It eats up the medical budget.

➢ Thence the fire spread along the hill, eating up houses, palaces, hanging gardens. According to a detailed estimate, the fire consumed some 2500 shops and 500 houses.

➢ The Dalai Lama once commented on how the culture in America is moving too fast, all of our conveniences eat up our time.

➢ The point is to push ourselves a little and discover what our time requirements really are. Calculate the cost of attending meetings. Meetings can eat up hours each week.

Similar expressions;

➢ To use up - to swallow - to consume - to wipe out - to deplete – to exhaust - to run through.

End up (doing)

Meaning; to finally be in a particular place or situation.

Examples;

➢ I was the one who had to make all of the decisions. When I left anything to him he screwed it up and I ended up fixing things to make them right.

➢ We gave you the best estimate we could but here's what it ended up costing and it ended up costing double what we said it was going to cost.

➢ They have not been adequately trained to perform any kind of police role, but, they end up doing police work.

➢ It took many negotiations across several years, but in the end both sides were pleased: the sanatorium men ended up with extra pay.

➢ While Terry is helping me, he begins to tell me his life story and how he ended up being in jail. It's a rotten system that allows such a person to end up in prison.

➢ She quickly fell into debt with the owners – to the point where she ended up working for them to pay off the debt she had accumulated.

Similar expressions;

➢ To finish up - to finish as - to result in.

Fall apart

Meaning;

1. To break up into pieces.
2. To fail; to stop working effectively; to not be able to cope.

Examples;

➤ After the sale talks fell apart, the company owners decided to rent it out.
➤ Whatever precautions we will take, we should always expect things to fall apart.
➤ My marriage fell apart as I was disappointed. Everything fell apart and I started to gain weight once more.
➤ As Jenny left me, my life started to fall apart and I decided to drop out of school.
➤ Given the choice between someone who tends to be easily stressed out by life and someone who tends to be calm and steady: choose the person less likely to fall apart.
➤ Without regular contacts, the project is likely to fall apart as partners lose interest or fail to keep to the agreed schedule: this might jeopardize the project.

Similar expressions;

1. To come apart - to disintegrate - to come to bits - to break apart – to decay - to perish - to go downhill - to go to ruin - to wear away.
2. To break down - to lose control - to malfunction - to hit bottom -to come to naught - to go wrong - to go astray - to cut off – to fall through.

Fall behind

Meaning: to not do something fast enough, or not do something by a particular time.

Examples;

➢ Local cinema could only remain dynamic as an artisan industry: it was bound to fall behind the technical advances in Europe and Latin America and it could not resist the aggressive global marketing, especially of the United States.

➢ Anybody –business or individual- who didn't keep up with technology was bound to fall behind and that included those who continued to rely on their dot-matrix printers.

➢ Quite often, recruiters and scouts tend to disregard the importance of academics by requesting to meet with athletes. As a result of these ill-advised meetings, the student ends up falling behind in class.

➢ The project has fallen behind schedule largely due to delays in completing the facilities' conceptual design and US funding constraints.

➢ Most large-scale construction projects fell behind schedule sooner or later, especially if there was a serious accident.

➢ Moerk told me she tutored some of the school's basketball players who fell behind in their studies because they spent much of their time practicing and traveling with the team.

Similar expressions;

➢ To not keep up - to not be getting anywhere - to lose out - to fall short – not to keep pace with – to hang back - to drop back.

Fall into (a/the) trap

Meaning: to get into difficult situation by doing something or trusting someone.

Examples;

➢ After some examination of reasons causing unproductivity, we found out that most coworkers too often fell into the trap of competition rather than standing by each other. Others turned out to be complacent.

➢ The biggest mistake I made was to take things for granted. I fell into the trap of letting my favorite pastime become part of my job until I lost interest and went out of business.

➢ Smith took care of his heart so well that he never fell in the trap of love.

➢ They intended me to fall into their trap when I showed them that I trusted them.

➢ It is I who am sorry. Once again I let myself fall into the trap of hope, and this time it was you who paid the price.

➢ Indeed, one of the biggest mistakes we can commit when encountering resistance is to fall into the trap of conversional obsession.

Similar expressions;

➢ To be the victim of - to be easy target of - to be easy prey - to be a sitting target.

Fall out

Meaning: to have an argument with.

Examples;

➤ Bill was totally tired of falling out with his parents all the time for no specific reasons.
➤ It was plain as day that Steve and Jane would fall out after that dinner.
➤ When we were younger, we used to fall out over borrowed clothes. When we got older, we started to fall out over television channels.
➤ Jenny fell out with Sally over cleaning their flat.
➤ Nobody expected that Sam's siblings would ever fall out over the inheritance.
➤ Elaine's friend lives over there, doesn't she? Overall, try not to fall out over children - I don't think it pays you, you only get resentful, don't you?

Similar expressions;

➤ To quarrel - to have a disagreement - to have a row - to have a fight - to be at odds - to get into a conflict - to have a difference of opinion.

Fed up with   -   Tired of   -   Sick of

Meaning: annoyed or bored by something that you have experienced for too long.

Examples;

➢ Mary got fed up with waiting for the mail under the scorching sunrays and left the line.

➢ Lucy travelled on her own because she's tired of her gossipy and unempathetic friends. She needed to take a break and to clear her head.

➢ They were tired of moving around and longed for a more stable lifestyle.

➢ I decided to set up my own business because I was sick of working at the mercy of others.

➢ I also needed kitchen basics, such as a fork. I was getting tired of scooping up the food with my fingers in the rancho.

➢ The moment you get tired of eating such a restricted diet and add some carbs back into your daily intake, the fat will cause you gain back weight.

➢ I was fed up! Completely, totally and utterly fed up. Fed up of always ending up at this same place where I am wrestling in my mind. Fed up of being so messed up inside.

Similar expressions;

➢ To be irritated - to be displeased - to be disgusted - to be frustrated - to be disgusted with - to be depressed.

Figure out - Find out

Meaning: to discover or find information about something.
- (figure out: understand – discover)

Examples;

- John is such an unpredictable and impulsive man – You can never figure out what he wants or will do.
- Can you figure out what's the capital of Italy without checking out your phone? It's as plain as day; Just use your head.
- It took me a while to find out how to install the battery and turn on the new phone.
- It was a complex topic. I couldn't figure out what the professor was talking about. My mind drifted away at the earliest few minutes.
- You are going to do me a great favor if you keep it between us; I don't want anyone to find out about what has happened.
- John appears to be in trouble after he defaulted on his repayments. Let's figure out some way to help him out and return some his past favors.
- Despite her attempts to conceal her relationship from her parents, somehow they found out that she was dating a police officer.

Similar expressions;

- To work out - to comprehend - to deduce - to make sense of something - to get the idea - to decipher - to digest - to get the picture - to make out someone - to identify with someone.

Fit in (with)

Meaning; to be convenient or accepted.

Examples;

➤ The party is in early June. How can that fit in with your holiday plans?

➤ The dentist can fit you in on Tuesday afternoon.

➤ He can fit in easily with other pupils in the class.

➤ New scientific findings or new scientific theories are true if they fit in With the accepted conceptual framework of the group.

➤ They all have in common certain traits: none fits in with the society surrounding her; none is initially interested in finding romantic love; none is initially interested in pursuing any particular goal.

➤ He also realizes that he needs to fit in and be part of the team. Between us, we've managed to create a look that fits in with his corporate lifestyle but also expresses his own unique personality.

Similar expressions;

➤ To be in harmony - to suit - to blend - to be convenient - to be acceptable - to be in line with - to accord - to match - to agree.

Flare up

Meaning: (for emotions or diseases) to become intense suddenly. when fire suddenly burns higher.

Examples;

- ➤ The speeding truck crashed into a wall and burst into flames. According to the passers-by, the driver survived by a miracle and was not hurt.
- ➤ Because of an engine malfunction. The plane burst into flames as it went off the runway.
- ➤ After the announcement of the results, my uncle would flare up whenever anyone mentions horses.
- ➤ The report indicated that her rash flared up because she went outdoors in the sunshine.
- ➤ We must be more cautious than before. Fires and storms could flare up again at any time.
- ➤ Even though I have never had to take another disability leave since starting my business, there were times when my symptoms would flare up.

Similar expressions;

- ➤ To blow up - to rage - to rise - to break out - to burst into flames - to blaze.

Freak out   -   Frighten /Scare someone to death

Meaning; to become very angry, frightened, or surprised, or to make someone do this.

Examples;

➢ I wish they removed this painting from the hall. It freaks me out for some reason I can't put my finger on.

➢ John took his sister shopping for a dress, and that freaked her out because she wasn't used to being treated well.

➢ The scene of rubbish bags and the rats freaked Jane out; she had trouble sleeping that night.

➢ As far as I knew the results of my tests hadn't been released yet. But my parents' weird looks freaked me out.

➢ I won't travel with Bill anymore. The way he drives scares me to death.

➢ Her weird looks scared the kids to death.

➢ Mary scared me to death when she passed out.

➢ His cutting words wounded her and frightened her to death.

Similar expressions;

➢ To break down - to lose one's mind - to lose one's cool - to go crazy - to blow one's mind - to terrify - to terrorize - to scare someone out of their mind - to scare the wits out of someone - to give someone the creeps - to give someone the shivers – to make someone's hair stand.

Get along with someone - Get on with someone

Meaning: to have a harmonious or friendly relationship.

Examples;

➢ Tom and Owen have always been getting on pretty well since their childhood, but they started to have arguments after the partnership.

➢ Mary got along well with her new roommates, and enjoyed their company.

➢ Don't fret about changing your department. People over there are all easy-going and easy to get on with.

➢ As Jessie moved into her new flat, she immediately found it really hard to get along with her new neighbors.

➢ You had better entitle Robin to deal with this issue. He is open-minded, friendly and gets on with everybody.

➢ There is a way to get along with people through a series of adjustments to your thinking and expectations. We are all different people and think in ways that may or may not agree with each other; however, we can still get along.

Similar expressions;

➢ To be friendly - to agree with - to be in harmony - to be on good terms - to be compatible - to be of the same mind/ opinion.

Get around

Meaning: to go or travel to different places.

Examples;

- ➢ I was wondering how difficult it is to get around if you don't speak the language. I did read that the sky-train in Bangkok had its stops announced in English, but haven't had much luck finding out anything else.
- ➢ Traffic congestion eliminates that advantage altogether by making it too hard to get around in a city. Too much trash turns city streets into a health hazard; too many drivers turn city streets into a parking lot.
- ➢ The City of Birmingham—not including suburbs—covers more than 150 square miles, and while there is limited bus service within the city and to some suburbs, the only real way to get around with any efficiency is by automobile.
- ➢ A good and extensive system of public transportation offers a variety of easy and economical ways to get around without getting bogged down in slow-moving Center City traffic and parking in expensive garages and lots.
- ➢ I primarily rely on mass transit to get around New York City and I find it the best way to navigate most of the neighborhoods I've profiled.
- ➢ People who do understand how to get around in a city without reference to the roads will be able to move faster on either attack or defense.

Similar expressions;

- ➢ To move around - to travel - to mobilize.

Get at someone/ something

Meaning:

1. **get access to** something. To reach or obtain something.
2. to try to suggest something without saying it directly.(allude)
3. to criticize someone.

Examples;

➤ Make sure you put the chocolate on the top shelf so that the children can't get at it.
➤ There is no way to get at the files unless Tom is here.
➤ What do you think that the author is getting at in these lines?
➤ Can you get to the point, please? I can't make out what you are getting at.
➤ No wonder your friends run away from you. People don't like being got at.
➤ We got used to the school principal getting at us every time we got late.

Similar expressions;

1. to touch - to pick up - to get to - to gain access to.
2. to imply - to hint - to mean - to intend - to lead up to - to point.
3. to pick on - to bully - to find fault with - to have a down on.

Get away with it

Meaning; to do something bad and not get punished or found out.

Examples;

➤ Tom did it again and didn't get punished. He's always getting away with his bad deeds.

➤ If dad has known about the neighbor's complaint, we won't get away with it this time.

➤ The police must have been paid off to turn a blind eye to Mrs. Kathy's accident. How in the world could she get away it so easily?

➤ He was still driving well into his seventies until he finally got caught. Amazingly, he got away with a caution, despite being well over the limit, but he was completely unrepentant about it.

➤ Was she going to let Liam, who had technically known her for about seven years, get away with calling her by completely the wrong name?

➤ We think it is worth examining that one in three emerging adults admits being prepared to violate the moral right or good if it helped them and they could get away with it.

Similar expressions;

➤ To escape blame /punishment for - to let off the hook - to go free - to slip away - to take flight - to fly the coop.

Get by (on/ with)

Meaning; to be able to live or deal with a situation with difficulty.

Examples;

➢ At that time I was very vigorous and active. I could only get by on only 5 hours of sleep – burning the candle at both ends.

➢ Tom is going through a very hard time these days. His income is really low and he is barely getting by.

➢ How can ten people get by on this tiny meal? This is just a drop in the ocean.

➢ We are trying to get by with this old computer until we come across a good offer to get a new one.

➢ I just know a few words in Japanese but I still can't get by.

➢ This office is too small for three people to get by.

Similar expressions;

➢ To manage - to cope - to scrape by/ through - to make ends meet - to get along - to barely have enough to live on - to scrimp.

Get/Be caught - Get/Be stuck

Meaning: to be unable to avoid something unpleasant or move further.

Examples;

➤ Mary was looking forward to a quiet and restful holiday but she got caught up in clearing out the garage throughout the weekend.

➤ Why are you bearing all this grudge against people. You are going to be caught up in your own schemes unless you adjust your attitude.

➤ Should you decide to risk trouble, you may not get caught right away. You may not get caught until the fourth time or maybe the seventh time you risk it, but the chances are, you will get caught sooner or later.

➤ The next time you are stuck in traffic, look at the people in the other cars. Although the suffering of others is generally not a source of humor, it is quite humorous watching how people respond to traffic.

➤ White reached down for his hand but couldn't span the distance. She took hold of the metal and pulled, but it wouldn't move. "I'm stuck!" he called again.

➤ Sometimes it's better to write a bad song than no song. Just keep at it. Don't force yourself, but do nudge yourself. If you get stuck and can't write, just write something.

Similar expressions;

➤ To be in the grip of - to be caught in the middle - to be chained to.

Get carried away - Go too far

Meaning; to become excited or involved in something that you lose control of your feelings or behavior. (go too far can also mean to exceed the limits)

Examples;

➢ Don't get too much carried away just because you are a bit smarter than the rest.

➢ Jane loved David as a brother, but he got carried away and truly fell in love with her.

➢ The drunk never remembered when he got carried away and wouldn't remember what he'd done the next day.

➢ As they ate, he listened very patiently when she got carried away describing all her gadgets from Williams-Sonoma, only laughing once.

➢ She was fearful of him at times but felt fairly secure that he would never go too far, or harm her, at least intentionally.

➢ I try to take care of my health because I think that the older people don't get the type of care they need. I try not to go too far because if I go too far, I might stress out and worry about things that you can't change.

➢ You can have fun and make everyone there have fun without taking chances or going too far. You are a professional.

Similar expressions;

➢ To lose self-control - to get excited - to get overexcited - to bite off too much - to take on too much - to overestimate - to exaggerate.

Get out of

Meaning; to avoid doing something that you should do, by giving an excuse.

Examples;

- It is easy to get into the mess, but it seems to take a life time to get out of it if you are that fortunate.
- She knew she'd behaved badly but she wondered now if he'd seen it as a way to get out of his commitment.
- It slipped means that the glass is responsible for its own falling. We don't just admit we did it. We pass the blame. We try to get out of responsibility. You are responsible for all of your experiences of life.
- The Doctor was saying that Lynda was nearing the end, and I wanted to be there for her, but I couldn't get out of attending the party.
- When most individuals realize they might suffer from the choices they've made, they'll do or say just about anything to get out of the mess they're in. Is it deviant, immoral, or unethical to try to circumvent pain with excuses?
- It's a matter of choice. I just starts exercise last year. Some days I almost made excuses to get out of it, but something always happens around me, reminding me that heart attacks can be avoided by exercise.

Similar examples;

- To slide out of - to evade - to shrink - to duck out of - to cop out of – to weasel out.

Get over

Meaning; to begin to feel better after being unhappy or ill.

Examples;

- ➤ It took her months to get over the shock of Richard leaving.
- ➤ Taking the attention of customers, product and/or service diversification, and focusing on marketing to get over the previous economic crises.
- ➤ Marshall had bragged to Ben about the damage he intended to do the Cowdens by violating Betty, but he would have to get over his weakness for her to accomplish that.
- ➤ She had never gotten over the helpless feeling of her father's betrayal and the finality of her loss. It was her punishment, she admitted, wiping her eyes and looking at the picture again.
- ➤ William was asleep in his bedroom at Balmoral when his father woke him with the news that his mother was dead. William and Harry have never got over the loss of their mother. To say they were devastated is inadequate.
- ➤ Skipper Mick Mills and the other survivors from the 1975 semi-final have still not really got over that defeat. It had a devastating effect on them. Their disappointment has got through to us.

Similar expressions;

- ➤ To look up - to get better - to get well - to bounce back - to get back on one's feet - to pull through - to shake off - to recover.

Get rid of (someone/something)

Meaning; to get free of someone or something; to dispose of or destroy.

Examples;

➤ Daddy kept looking after the other plants and vegetables – pulling the weeds out, getting rid of the snails that were trying to eat the strawberries, and watering the garden.

➤ You may be able to get rid of him without even letting him know that he was not the right person for you.

➤ "Turns out he did actually get caught a few months ago, but they decided to get rid of the associate who reported him instead of sacking him!"

➤ To get rid of these diseases, one should give up these harmful habits. Even if these habits are given up, the body needs some time to become normal and heal the damage.

➤ In order to do it well, we have to get rid of the clutter that would otherwise hold us back. So get rid of these things. Don't give them any space in your life.

➤ Most people put much more energy into trying to manage their fears than they do trying to identify the cause and get rid of them for good.

Similar expressions;

➤ To do away with - to throw away - to throw out - to dismiss - to expel - to get shut of - to root out - to eliminate - to wipe out - to kill - to destroy.

Get hold of someone   -   Get in touch with someone

Meaning: to contact someone.

✓   **Opposite**; (to be) Out of touch with/ Lose touch with.

Examples;

➢ Where on earth have you been man? I have been trying to get hold of you all morning.

➢ Martin is always on the move. It's almost impossible to get hold of him.

➢ After years of travel, I wasn't able to get hold of any of my old team members. Most of them got married; others left the country.

➢ Jane wasn't able to get in touch with her family after the storm.

➢ For any inquiry, please don't hesitate to get in touch with us.

➢ After Steve got into business, he was out of sight and out of touch.

➢ As you expand, be sure that your customer service remains the same (or improves), and that you do not lose touch with your customers.

➢ We stayed in touch for about two years, mostly through Christmas cards and typical correspondence. Then I got married, moved away and we lost touch with each other. I always remembered Jill and kept her picture with my others.

Similar expressions;

➢ To communicate with - to be in touch with - to call - to contact - to reach - to phone - to touch base.

Get on

Meaning; to go onto a bus, train, aircraft, or boat.

✓ **Opposite: Get off**

Examples;

➢ In the dream, I was getting on a very slow-moving bus that frequently stopped to let passengers off. For reasons unknown, I was sitting on top of the bus and noticed that no other passengers were getting on.

➢ My perspective is a little different from the Passengers because the Passengers are only on the bus for a short time. The Passengers get on the bus and when the bus gets to their destination they get off the bus.

➢ You usually can get on a boat at the last minute. However, it is better to buy your ticket two or three days ahead if you are travelling between July 15 and August 30.

➢ I left the car in the three-hour car park. The wife was going to pick it up after work, but when I got on the train I found the spare keys in my pocket.

➢ So we just walked down the steps to the train tracks. We got on a train that felt to us like the right one. The fourth man got on with us. He looked like a typical Russian man. He said nothing to us. We got off the train when it stopped.

➢ When the plane left New York, there were 110 people on board plus 15 crew members. The plane stopped in Chicago. 46 people got off the plane. 57 passengers plus two more crew members got on the plane.

Similar expressions;

➢ To embark - to ascend - to climb - to mount - to hop - to take.

Get through

Meaning;

1. to manage to deal with a difficult situation until it is over.
2. to be connected to a place by telephone.

Examples;

- ➤ I couldn't get through – the line was engaged. But I finally got through to Warren on his mobile.
- ➤ She was relying on luck to get her through.
- ➤ He needs a lot of coffee to get him through the day.
- ➤ I just have to get through the first five minutes of my speech, and then I'll be fine.
- ➤ The refugees will need help to get through the winter.
- ➤ I tried to phone him back the day after he left the message but I couldn't get through. I left messages for him but he never returned my calls.
- ➤ They stepped into the elevator as Shaun tried to contact Parsons on the walkie-talkie, but the thick metal walls that lined the elevator shaft made it difficult for the signal to get through.
- ➤ It was early evening and snow fell heavily while Anna held her children's hands tightly trying hard to get through the crowded streets quickly without losing one of them.

Similar expressions;

1. To overcome - to cope with - to carry off - to go through - to handle.
2. To reach - to get in touch - to get to - to contact - to approach.

Get up

Meaning; to stand up; rise or cause to rise from bed after sleeping.

Examples;

➢ The whole audience got up and started clapping as soon as the president entered the hall.

➢ Jessie was convinced that there was more to the stories, and she had a hard time believing that Abigail could just up and leave her father. I got up to switch off the radio when, all at once, the door swung open.

➢ I remember the weatherman saying it was going to be a windy and snowy winter, but all was calm that Christmas morning. I got up before everyone else and went downstairs.

➢ The ride up to their house in Marin County made me carsick, due to the sharp turns through Samuel P. Taylor Park. Their yells seemed to annoy Fay and all at once she got up to go put the dishes in the automatic dishwater.

➢ It's getting dark. He said he wanted to cross the Long River to Wuchang and visit a friend. They arrived in the ferry but ZHANG did not get up immediately. Until the iron gate in the ferry entrance was going to shut.

➢ I told myself when my alarm clock went off that if I didn't get up immediately my day would not be as productive as it could be.

Similar expressions;

➢ To stand (up) - to rise - to get to your feet.

Give away

Meaning:

1. to give something to someone without asking for any money.
2. to tell information or facts that you should keep secret.

Examples;

➢ To promote the book, they're giving away a CD with every copy.
➢ A large percentage of the proceeds will be given away to a cancer awareness charity.
➢ As winter is just around the corner. I think we'd better give some coats away.
➢ I gave away all the plants that were left in our garden to neighbors. They know how to look after them.
➢ The party was meant to be a surprise, but Caroline spilt the beans and gave it away.
➢ Far from it. Jane is very careful – she's the last person to give away such a secret.
➢ If you don't want your family to know about your marriage, don't give yourself away by spending too much time out.

Similar expressions;

1. to present - to yield - to distribute - to bestow - to dole out - to donate - to gift - to endow.
2. to reveal - to let on - to disclose - to let it slip - to spill the beans – to blow the gaff - to confide - to go public.

Give off

Meaning; to produce something such as heat, light, or a smell.

Examples;

➤ When they die, plants give off gases such as carbon dioxide and methane.

➤ Heat energy makes things feel hot. Heat energy from one object can move to another object. Heat is a type of energy that makes temperatures warm up. Everything gives off heat.

➤ Regular light bulbs haven't changed a whole lot since Thomas Edison invented them in 1879; they're basically mini-heaters that give off light as a byproduct.

➤ The fire uses up the oxygen that you need to breathe and gives off smoke and poisonous gases that even a small amount taken in to your lungs can make you disoriented and drowsy.

➤ A liquid or solid substance which on contact with fire or when exposed to air gives off dangerous or intensely irritating fumes.

➤ Harmful gases cause acid rain Some factories, specially power plants where coal is burnt to make electricity, give off certain harmful gases.

Similar expressions;

➤ To send out - to emit - to discharge - to give out - to generate - to fume - to leak - to pump out - to release.

Give up

Meaning: to stop doing something that you do regularly; admit defeat.

Examples;

➤ After ten minutes trying to get the answer I gave up.

➤ She has a struggle trying to persuade the board to accept her proposal, but she's determined not to give up.

➤ Ester had tried dieting and even exercising but he eventually gave up when he realized it was a futile effort. Plus, now that he was in a committed relationship, he didn't care how he looked.

➤ Seeing the odds entirely against us in numbers, and having gained the great victory, we gave up without resistance, and suffered ourselves to be arrested by the sheriff's posse.

➤ My vision for the future is stronger than any struggles or setbacks I face in the present because I know the surest way to succeed lies in never giving up. No matter how long it takes or how hard I have to work.

➤ You can learn from my life experiences. No matter how many doors are slammed in my face, I will never give up, because I'm the one responsible for making my dreams a reality.

Similar expressions;

➤ To admit defeat - to concede defeat - to stop trying - to call it a day - to give in - to surrender - to capitulate - to be beaten - to despair - to lose heart - to abandon hope - to quit.

Go for (it - something)

Meaning: said to encourage someone to do something.

Examples;

➢ Tom: "I think I have to get this phone. I have got enough of mine."
Sarah:" Why the delay? Go for it."

➢ I'm looking forward to getting into business and my dad is encouraging me to go for it.

➢ It doesn't take a genius to figure out how to make success. You should learn how to set a reasonable goal and to go for it.

➢ Just" go for it". Easier said than done. The truth was, even as she said that, Della realized she did feel better. She felt as if a huge weight had been lifted from her shoulders.

➢ We'll just go for it, like you said. And we'll take what we get. If there's something wrong with the baby, we'll handle it when it happens.

➢ The process of preparing for an audition begins long before the actual audition day. Some people think, "I'm just going to go for it." That's fine, but go for it after you prepare. Going for it after you've prepared is just as exciting and exhilarating as winning it.

Similar expressions;

➢ Not to hesitate – to go ahead - to go on - no pain no gain - to give it a try.

Go over

Meaning: to consider, examine or check something.

Examples;

➤ It seems I am not with it. Can I give today's rehearsal a miss? I can't even go over my lines.

➤ Let's go over each item of the instructions once more for more clarity and precision.

➤ What is holding us back is that some students rush to hand out their assignments without going over their work.

➤ I spent the entire weekend going over the report word by word trying to locate the flaw but to no avail.

➤ It makes more sense to keep everything in perspective and not sweat over the minor stuff. Let's go over our objectives and priorities.

➤ Sarah is going over the details of the examination to work out what went wrong.

Similar expressions;

➤ To review - to study - to inspect - to read over - to look at / over - to analyze - to rehearse - to practice.

Go through

Meaning:

1. to experience a difficult or unpleasant situation.
2. to examine the contents of something to find something.

Examples;

➤ Even though our family went through many financial crises, we refused to sell any of our properties.

➤ At the check-in a customs officer went through my suitcase and handed the phone back to me.

➤ Why don't you get down to work and give us a hand? It will take ages to go through all these e-mails on our own.

➤ Although we go through all kinds of challenges life brings our way, we're in it together and I cherish each day I have with him.

➤ I must be losing my mind, Kate thought. I could have sworn I'd brought it down. Oh well, I must have packed it. Now I'll have to go through all those darn boxes looking for it.

➤ You have to go through all the steps to arrive at the milestones along the way. There are so many people who don't even arrive at this level during a whole lifetime, and you're only 26.

Similar expressions;

1. to undergo - to experience - to suffer - to live through - to endure – to bear - to tolerate - to withstand - to put up with - to sustain.
2. to search - to look through - to turn inside out - to check - to inspect – to read over - to look over - to review.

Go up

Meaning:

1. to move higher, rise, or increase. **(go down: decrease).**
2. to suddenly explode.
3. if a building goes up, it is built.

Examples;

- ➢ A new factory is going up at the site of the old airport.

- ➢ There's a gas leak and the whole building could go up at any moment.

- ➢ The area has recently become very fashionable and house prices are going up.

- ➢ Train fares are expected to go up by 10 % again.

- ➢ When the rockets went up that evening, the crowd panicked and raced for the entrance to the Underground.

- ➢ He brought many workers and the bridge went up very quickly. The mayor began to worry when there was an hour before down and the bridge was almost complete.

Similar expressions;

1. To build up - to move up - to come up - to pile up - to soar - to mount.
2. To blow up - to go off - to erupt - to go boom - to set off.
3. To put up - to construct - to set up.

Hang around/out

Meaning: to spend time with someone usually without doing much.

Examples;

- Dogs of the same street bark alike. Hanging out with those punks means picking up their bad habits.
- Jane is leading such a carefree life. She has nothing to do other than hanging around the shopping center down the street with her friends.
- Signs are posted around the building to indicate the location, and everyone meets at the local bar of choice to have fun and hang out.
- Randal was picking up a gambling habit and was hanging around with some dangerous folks that were making him a victim of loan sharks.
- Lawyers can learn a lot hanging around a barbershop. Watch folks come in, see what they pick up from the magazine rack.
- In the afternoons, after work, I'd hang around Pauper's reading the paper and sipping free drinks while Lola worked.

Similar expressions;

- To keep company with - to go around - to socialize - to spend time - to rub shoulders.

Hang up

Meaning;

1. to finish a conversation on the telephone.
2. to put something such as a coat somewhere where it can hang.

Examples;

➤ Dinner was always about 6:30 pm she would rush in the door, and hang her keys up by the door.

➤ After Justin hangs up his coat, the music therapist immediately takes the coat picture, substitutes it with another that represents the next activity, and begins singing about this next event on his classroom schedule.

➤ Take the beef out of the pan, dry it with a cloth, strew flour on it, and hang it up in a moderate warm place to dry.

➤ I always speak with people that think if they say, "I'm sorry" or "No thank you" it's perfectly ok to hang up while I'm still talking.

➤ They talked a while longer and were about to hang up when janet reminded her of the near accident they had as they left the park that morning.

➤ I'll write you a note to fix a meeting for the middle of next week, the fact is I need you, Dr. Pereira, I need your support. Please excuse me, I'm calling from somewhere very inconvenient and I have to hang up. 'Get lost!' she shouted, and hung up on me.

Similar expressions;

1. To cut off - to put the phone down - to shut - to block.
2. To suspend - to dangle - to hang out/ to air - to hang down.

Hold back

Meaning: to stop something or someone from moving, developing or being successful.

Examples;

➢ Sweat was in my eyes and dirt was stuck to me everywhere. My dry lips was salty from the sweat. I climbed. I never doubted that I could make it, but what held me back was this hefty bag I carried on my back.

➢ Some of the factors that held us back were understandable. Yet they were mishandled, and that led us to wrong conclusions and unwise courses of action.

➢ The only thing that can hold us back is our thoughts. This planet and its blessings are ours to experience and enjoy, the miracle of ourselves to unravel.

➢ We hoped to be in Fiji by the time this event came around, so as to fly back to Maine. There were too many delays that held back our well-intended plans.

➢ I was starting out fresh, and nothing would hold me back. I opened my eyes. The campus was nestled on the eastern side of New York.

➢ What would your life be like if you could achieve anything you set your mind on? Absolutely nothing would hold you back and you would be able to move ahead quickly and smoothly.

Similar expressions;

➢ To prevent - to restrain - to stop - to tie one's hands - to suppress - to withhold - to delay - to back off - to back out - to pull out - to clip one's wings.

Hold on

Meaning:

1. to wait or stop.
2. to endure in difficult circumstances.

Examples;

➤ Hold on here for a minute - it seems I've left the keys in the office. I won't be long.

➤ You want to know where the event will take place. Alright, hold on a sec. I need to check my diary out.

➤ It takes a bit of patience to get the tangible results of our plan. Just hold on, and everything will be all right.

➤ Sarah's calls have driven me crazy. Why doesn't she hold on a bit longer? What's the hurry?

➤ We took great pains to get our company off the ground. We managed to hold on through some hard times.

➤ Take courage Mark! Hold on just a bit more - the ambulance is on the way.

Similar expressions;

1. Wait a minute - just a minute /a moment/ a second - stay here - remain here - hang on - sit tight - hold your horses.
2. To keep on - to carry on - to hang on - to stay the course – to stick it out- to stick at it - to persevere - to last.

Hold up

Meaning;

1. To make someone or something late or prevent from doing.
2. To remain stable, strong or in a good condition.

Examples;

➢ Sorry for being late, the bus was held up for half an hour because of a technical issue.

➢ I'm saying it boldly; the dispute must be resolved and the peace process mustn't be held up any longer.

➢ Clare got held up at work at the request of her director as they were falling far behind schedule.

➢ There are increasing fears that our team may not hold up for the finals after the last defeat.

➢ The data shows that prices had help up until the year 2000.

➢ Don't worry. Our house is equipped well to hold up during natural disasters.

➢ All of the players except Ken said, "Sure, we'll hold up play till you get back," but Ken refused.

Similar expressions;

1. To delay - to put off - to postpone - to pause - to slow down - to interrupt - to interfere.
2. To maintain - to withstand - to stabilize - to level off - to preserve – to regularize - to standardize.

Keep/ Carry on (doing)

Meaning: to continue to do something, or to do something again and again.

Examples;

➤ Turn left at the corner and keep on. As you get the traffic intersection, give me a call.

➤ She kept on trying to pick it up while the ranger kept on trying to take it away from her. It sure looked like a battle going on between them.

➤ I kept on practicing day and night, trying to be a master gun shooter. Then I called myself the cowboy.

➤ There are more reasons (and better reasons) for you to quit smoking than to carry on smoking. Yet you still smoke, why? Because, you have linked good thoughts, beliefs, and feelings towards smoking.

➤ If you have already signed a contract with the first client, service ethics should tell you to carry on with the first job even if you won't make much money.

➤ Such irresponsible and hostile acts don't encourage employees to carry out active policies concerning work and health nor do they encourage them to carry on working or return to work quickly if necessary.

➤ To hear myself called 'dear' by such a beautiful hand, dictated by such a pretty mouth, I can take it no longer! If I carry on reading, I'll collapse to the floor. This letter is an inferno for me! I can't read it any longer. I must tear it up.

Similar expressions;

➤ To go on - to persist in - to persevere in - to keep going with - to go ahead.

Keep at (something) - Keep up (something)

Meaning:

- (keep at): to continue working hard at something difficult. To persist.
- (keep up): keep something in an efficient or proper state.

Examples;

- ➢ Learning a language is worth the effort and it is much easier and enjoyable than most people believe, but you've got to keep at it.
- ➢ If you keep at it, sooner or later it will work. Just take full responsibility and don't be a quitter.
- ➢ The cards did not break his way, but he kept at it – and then kept at it some more. By the end of the evening, Lasker owed 500 bucks.
- ➢ While pointing out the impact takes a bit of time and is not as easy as simply saying "good job," it goes a long way towards helping others. Use direct language and encourage people to keep up the good work.
- ➢ You've made it this far; so you've probably made great strides toward living a determined, targeted life. Keep it up. Keep standing tall, no matter what.
- ➢ The challenge is not to grow weary in your efforts in shaping the child. If you have done your job well, you should be inspired to keep it up.

Similar expressions;

- ➢ To show determination in - to keep going with - not to give up - to persist with - to persevere with - to stick at.

Keep up/pace with

Meaning; to move or develop at the same speed as someone or something else.

✓ **Opposite**: Lose track of.

Examples;

➢ Students need to be acquainted with ways to keep pace with life as well as with their fellows.
➢ When prices rise, people worry whether the rise in their income will keep pace with inflation and retain the purchasing power of their money.
➢ Some countries made small unimportant steps towards keeping pace with globalization.
➢ Losing track of how fast you are driving is no excuse for speeding.
➢ She was obsessed with keeping up to date with the cell phones that have most features, keeping up with video games and with new design trends.
➢ It is an endless challenge, which I gladly accept, to keep up with the extraordinary abundance of food products.
➢ Can you stop talking for a minute? I'm losing track of where I am in the movie.
➢ Jack, being a police sergeant, and one of the old school soon made it clear that he was taking charge and wanted to be kept up to date with anything and everything that happened or was discovered, or more survivors found.

Similar expressions;

➢ To keep step - to pace - to equate - to match.

Keep/ Hold/ Sit/ Stand still

Meaning; used to tell someone not to move. To stay motionless.

Examples;

➢ The crisis brought our business and cash flow to a standstill for over than three weeks.

➢ Some birds can keep still in the air. What do they stand on? If space contains only air, birds would not be able to stand still.

➢ A rolling stone gathers no moss. To find true happiness, never hold still. Having got a job seems enough for most people that they will just do it and thus remain static for the rest of their lives.

➢ The time needed to bring the system to a standstill is a monotone decreasing function.

➢ Hold still, son! Give me a chance to check out what this red spot on your forehead is.

➢ When 16-mm films are shown, the students are expected to hold still and remain quiet, thus a passive viewing posture is enforced.

Similar expressions;

➢ Stand still: knock it off - hold it - stop it - give it a rest.
➢ Standstill (noun): halt – stop - dead stop - stand.

Knock down

Meaning; to hit someone or something forcefully so that they fall down.

Examples;

➢ When a contestant has been knocked down, the referee will order the standing contestant to the farthest neutral corner.

➢ Kate loves bowling. When she rolls the ball, it doesn't always travel straight to knock down all the pins.

➢ You want to set them up in a way that after you knock down the first domino, all the dominos will eventually fall.

➢ We are often set back or knocked down by those who seek to harm us, and sometimes their devices knock them down. Harm seek harm find.

➢ Within hours, they knocked down five buildings and leveled them off.

➢ The crowd went wild and started knocking down the seats, the tables and everything comes up in their way.

Similar expressions;

➢ To pull down - to destroy - to crush - to smash - to level - to crack - to wipe off - to take apart.

Lay someone off

Meaning; to stop employing someone. Or stop doing something.

Examples;

➤ Officials who refused to carry out the orders would themselves be laid off. Ten percent of the workers would be dismissed by January.

➤ But what happens if the job offer is from a company that is actually laying off employees? How smart is it to take a job there?

➤ But sometimes the pressures got to be too much. Just like tomorrow, when she had to tell Sandy that she would have to lay her off.

➤ The company had to lay off lots of people because of the hard time it is going through. There is no one to blame if you are laid off.

➤ Maybe you've been worried about the prospect of getting laid off, and now you're relieved that the axe has finally fallen.

➤ Her seniority set the pay rate, so management would be pleased to lay her off for any reason, and replace her with a lower-wage earner.

Similar expressions;

➤ To dismiss - to fire - to let go - to oust - to fire - to kick out - to show the door - to sack - to boot out – to get rid of.

Leave out

Meaning: to not include someone or something.

Examples

➤ If information does not appear clear, then the chances are that it really did not make sense to you anyway. You may either rework it to make it clear or leave it out entirely, provided it is not information critical to your study.

➤ No one has to be left out to feel left out; a person simply has to believe that the bonds between others are more alive or intense or intimate than their connection with him.

➤ They had dedicated themselves to work, to money, spending their time on acquiring life and things, but had left out the most important part. While they loved each other, never being selfish, they had no legacy, no children to fill the home.

➤ I could've listed many more movements here, but I listed the ones I think are the most effective. I left out all the ones I don't like, like lunges, for example.

➤ Let's leave her out of this, shall we? There are things you don't know and until you're my age and have walked in my shoes then you'll never understand.

➤ I think it would be best to leave that part out for the time being, Mom. The family is in danger as it is, and I don't know how bad this will get.

Similar expressions;

➤ Exclude – except - leave off – omit - take out – eliminate - get rid of - do away with – neglect – pretermit – drop – miss – overlook - overleap.

Let (someone) down

Meaning: to disappoint someone by failing to do what you agreed to do.

Examples;

➢ Jaime slept next to me in the dark, her face nestled into the green nylon of her sleeping bag. I was staring at her trying to convince myself that she is my biggest ally and won't let me down.

➢ What disappointed me was that my dad let me down although he said that he loved me a lot.

➢ Once, not so long ago, he was one of us. We respected him as our leader. Although he let us down, let's respect him in death.

➢ Life may let us down; our friends may let us down; our family may let us down, but Allah never does. His love is limitless and his care is endless.

➢ I shouldn't have relied upon her father who had a bunch of friends who were horrible characters. I feel like I let her down when she really needed me beside her.

➢ They have been working to support you all of their lives. Now don't neglect them in their old age. Don't let your parents down; they brought you up!

Similar expressions;

➢ To disappoint - to fail to support - to leave stranded - to leave high and dry - to stab in the back - to betray - to bail on.

Let off

Meaning;

1. not punish someone or not punish severely.
2. to excuse someone from a task or obligation.

Examples;

➢ The judge let her off with a warning and a fine instead of a prison sentence.
➢ My Mum said I had to do all the ironing as a punishment, but I'm hoping she'll let me off.
➢ Considering the severity of the crime, they were let off lightly.
➢ I let him off because he seemed so sorry and promised not to lie to me again.
➢ I asked the captain to let me off at the next port of call.
➢ The theatre management kindly let me off a couple of performances to go to Yorkshire.
➢ I'll bring him myself next week, on my way to work, and I'll collect him on the way home, but after that I'd like him to take the bus. I've told the hospital where I work about the situation, and they've let me off night shifts for three months.

Similar expressions;

1. To pardon - to forgive - to grant an amnesty - to release - to discharge - to be lenient on/to - to be merciful to - to have mercy on - to acquit.
2. To excuse from - to relieve from - to exempt from - to spare from

Let out

Meaning:

1. (of a class or school) to end or be finished.
2. to allow a person or animal to leave a place.

Examples;

➢ Often during Catechism class time, my buddies and I would sneak out to the local drug store for candy only to get back in time for the teacher to let out class!

➢ It opened up into a courtyard and there was an empty picnic table where we could hang out and wait for the class to let out.

➢ There are only about five or six weeks left of school. I'm sure it wouldn't be a big deal." "Yes it would, Mitchell. School lets out at three o'clock.

➢ We all looked at each other knowing that Noah will not let us out unless he is certain that it is safe.

➢ Let me take a quick look at it, and I think you need to let the kids out of the car before they pass out; inside's too hot for them, even with the windows down.

➢ She ran straight to the barn as soon as I let her out, with her nose to the ground. Clever girl.

Similar expressions;

1. To end - to finish - to close - to wind up.
2. To let loose - to unwrap - to let on - to bring out - to let go of - let go - release.

Level off/ out

Meaning; to stop rising or falling and stay at the same level.

Examples;

➢ The road levels out before starting to drop through a gateway and then swinging sharply to the right.

➢ The proportion of unemployed graduates increased sharply from the 1980s to the 1990s and then levelled off over the following two decades.

➢ Diabetes death rate increased and then levelled out during the first half of this century.

➢ This season's revenues are growing steadily, reaching over $2 billion. Similarly, the rising costs levelled off around $1.5 billion.

➢ Classroom participation rates are rising noticeably this term, after a long time of levelling off.

➢ The temperature is leveling out for the time being. But it is expected to drop gradually in the next few days.

Similar expressions;

➢ To stabilize - to settle down - to even out - to steady - to smooth out.

Look after

Meaning; to take care of someone or something.

Examples;

➤ There are so many websites out there to learn how to look after your health in general and your teeth in particular.

➤ Jenny has taken it upon herself to look after her sister while her mother is out tomorrow.

➤ It was a dreadful experience to look after Bill's puppy when he went away. That disobedient creature burned me out totally.

➤ Upstanding companies know how to look after their customers and keep them satisfied.

➤ Jason is such a noble man. He retired three years in advance to look after his ill wife.

➤ David's friends were always willing to look after his flowers and plants when he was out of town.

Similar expressions;

➤ To care for - to attend to - to take charge of - to keep an eye on - to watch over - to keep safe - to nurse - to babysit - to protect - to guard.

Look back

Meaning: to remember something in the past.

Examples;

➤ He looked back on his childhood with affection.

➤ Looking back on my life, I recognize that learning has always been the wellspring of discovery and insight for me.

➤ I look back at my party life and see just how much time I lost. I look back at the people I tried to be like and I still feel unique. I look back on all the people I've dated and none of them made me feel complete.

➤ It was over and done with and there is no point in looking back at the past when there is living to do in the present'.

➤ When I was growing up way back in the forties and fifties the town had just about everything a kid could need. As I look back on things at that time I believe that there was a stabilizing influence on the community.

➤ When we look back at the times that we "stepped out" to do our own thing, can we truly say our desires were fulfilled?

Similar examples;

➤ To retrospect - to call to mind - to recall - to recollect - to think back - to summon up - to bring to mind - to call up - to go back - to flash on - to dig into the past - to review in retrospect.

Look forward to (doing)

Meaning; to feel happy and excited about something that is going to happen.

Examples;

➢ I truly value the opportunity to participate in this workshop and I look forward to continuing to work with you on this important topic.

➢ I'm looking forward to the bus ride! It will probably be really nice! Looking forward to visiting cities where we can go shopping.

➢ Every time I crossed the finish line, I was already looking forward to the next training season and the next race.

➢ I have always looked forward to Mondays, but not everyone does. If you dread Monday, you may need some change in your weekly routine.

➢ I look forward to working with the administration to learn the details of these proposals in the near future.

➢ Children and even some adults love this time before Christmas because it gives them something for which to look forward and feel overjoyed.

Similar expressions;

➢ To hope for - to be prepared for - to count on - to await - to lick one's lips.

Look across/ over

Meaning; to have a view of a certain area.

Examples;

➢ This view looks across the lake toward the dam, which was designed as an arched bridge to give the impression that the lake continues on the other side, but in fact it disguises a spillway forming a double cascade.

➢ What little light there was came through the soot-blackened glass of the rear room, what the landlord called the "parlor." There was a small window in the kitchen that looked across to another small window in a brick wall.

➢ As we sat at a big table in a room looking over the river in Marshfield, his wife Nakote brought coffee and cake, and I heard the story of his mill. Their house, next to the mill, is as close to the river as you can get and stay dry.

➢ In her large, long, rather low-ceilinged study whose casement windows looked over the river, sat Stephen.

➢ It was true that the window looked over the village high street, but the street was only a pile of rubble and rubbish.

➢ The rear windows looked over the yard on to the red brick wall of a four-story woolen mill, its hammered glass windows thick with grime.

Similar expressions;

➢ To overlook - to have a view of - afford a view of - look on to - look out on/over - face - front on to - give on to - give over - open out over - command a view of – dominate.

Make up

Meaning;
1. to reconcile.
2. to say or write something that is not true.
3. to form.
4. (make up for): to replace something lost or damaged or to compensate

Examples;

➤ Some began to make up excuses to get out of the night shift.

➤ If you are going to make up another story, do me a favor and keep it to yourself. Honestly, I've got enough of your made-up stories.

➤ He'd screwed everything up. But he went back with a bouquet of flowers to make it up with Maggie. He wanted make amends for his atrocious behavior.

➤ Sarah apologized to Emilie for not being a better aunt saying; "Please, give me the chance to make it up to you; I didn't mean to ignore you!"

➤ The individuals who make up the team must become aware of the assumptions they make, the choices they enact and the behavior they exhibit.

➤ This panel, Asian in style and made up of complex mixture of vegetation.

➤ I'd rather to give the picnic a miss. I'm taking extra lessons to make up for the time I missed.

Similar expressions;

1. To come to terms - to make peace - to shake hands - to settle.
2. To create - to compose - to fabricate - to fake it - to pretend.
3. To be a member of - to be made of - to comprise - to consist of.
4. To make amends/recompense for - to atone - to balance - to expiate.

Make up one's mind   -   Take a decision

Meaning: to decide.

Examples;

➢ Many times she had made up her mind to discuss this issue with Nil, but her courage had never as yet mounted high enough to do so.

➢ Made up his mind more quickly about his conclusions regarding me, maybe because, as he said, I talked a lot with my hands.

➢ I don't like changing my routine for other people, once I make up my mind I stick to it. When in disagreement, I tend to listen with my mind made up.

➢ A project manager is not authorized to take an investment decision, due to his position in the organizational structure.

➢ It's useful to use a maximizing process in order to make a decision.

➢ We can't very well solve practical problems or make good decisions without taking some risks. You gotta crack a few eggs to make an omelet.

Similar expressions;

➢ To come to a decision - to reach a decision - to settle on a plan of action - to come to a conclusion - to reach a conclusion.

Measure up - Up to scratch/standard

Meaning; to be good enough to meet a standard.

Examples;

- Nermey also made it clear that he would take away the jobs of leaders who don't measure up.
- I wanted this as much as they did, but I still felt a lot of pressure to measure up to their expectations.
- If your total income does not measure up to the amount you need to maintain your lifestyle, it helps if you have your documentation in place.
- Every effort must be made through continuing research to bring the record up to scratch.
- It took years of hard work and research before we got up to scratch to meet Pan Am's high standards.
- If a vegetable did not come up to standard, Stephan would reject it and these vegetables would be placed in a pile in one side in the greenhouse for the apprentices to cook during mealtimes.
- In commercial documents or otherwise that a product is 'up to standard'. A regulator or specifier who suspects that it is not up to standard can have it tested.

Similar expressions;

- Measure up: to meet the requirements - to amount to - to come up to – to rank with - to level - to cope with.
- Up to scratch: up to standard - up to the mark - up to par.

Mess around

Meaning;
1. to waste time;
2. to behave badly or in a silly way.

Examples;

➢ When the alarm fire went off, we were in front of the building messing around and telling jokes.
➢ Owen seems to be in serious trouble. He was messing around with a girl who turned out to be the sister of a police officer.
➢ Everyone in the hall was telling us not to mess around, though they themselves did.
➢ She kept messing around throughout the weekend, in an attempt to ease off her concerns and fears about the sale of her house.
➢ They wanted me to monitor the students' work and walk around them, to tell them not to mess around or to ask questions.
➢ You had no business to mess around with that man. You created your own mess and now you want to blame somebody for it.

Similar expressions;

➢ To mess about - to fiddle - to play around - to muck around - to pass the time - to toy.

Mess up

Meaning; to spoil something, or to mishandle a situation.

Examples;

➢ This project is messed up! I'm late! I can't remember everything that I have to do! Everything is a mess! I can't figure this out! I'm late!

➢ There are a million stupid things people do to mess up their recovery; unaware that they are self-destructive.

➢ This message is kind of a wake-up call to young people. Some effective methods to help them overcome their difficulties if their life has been messing up.

➢ Gan promised to have the papers delivered to him before midday Monday as a peace offering for having messed up this weekend.

➢ To clean up the mess, they decided to attack individuals who messed up nature; spotted owls and polar bears.

➢ She took the boys into the backyard and set up the lawn sprinkler. She was confident of them because she taught them to admit when they messed up.

Similar expressions;

➢ To ruin - to confuse - to screw up - to mix up – to spoil - to disorder - to disorganize - to unbalance.

Move in/ out

Meaning;

1. (move in) to begin living in a new home.
2. (move out) to stop living in a particular home.

Examples;

➤ When one of the tenants move out and the other tenants stay, you need to do a few things to keep your records straight.

➤ Most Americans first move out of their parents' household at age 18 or 19, usually either to go away to college or simply to be independent.

➤ I moved out of my mum's place and then into a flat above a bar, which obviously didn't suit me much. The noise over there messed with my head.

➤ Clare moved to a two-bedroom flat waiting for Lisa to give her the green light to move in with her.

➤ We moved to South Carolina in 2009. When we first arrived, we moved into a rental home, later on I was able to find employment with a local garden store.

➤ As the original owners retired and moved to sunnier climates, young professionals moved in and updated the place.

Similar expressions;

1. to inhabit - to settle - to reside - to set up home.
2. to move away - to resettle - to leave – to depart.

Move on/ ahead

Meaning; to advance and go forward.

Examples;

➢ Regardless of the circumstances, as humans, we have to learn to move ahead while focusing our minds on our targets.

➢ Grief is real, the grief process can be long and involved , and those who are stuck in the process may need help moving ahead.

➢ That car must move on to allow space for other cars to enter and exit. Who on earth is its careless owner?

➢ Moving on to the main point, the defaulters have many questions to answer about the damage they caused.

➢ This workbook will provide you with a road map to deal with all levels and ages of children when you are moving ahead.

➢ If you moved on from the exercise without completing it, I challenge you to go back and complete it. It won't take you long, but its insights for you could be helpful.

Similar expressions;

➢ To go ahead - to continue.

Name after

Meaning; to give someone or something the same name as someone or something else.

Examples;

- Element 95 was named americium after its country of discovery because of its chemical similarity to europium which was named after Europe.
- The planet Saturn is named after thee Roman god of seedtime and harvest. And the planet Venus is named after the Roman goddess of love.
- The Caesar salad is not named for Julius Caesar, it's named for its creator, Caesar Cardini.
- Most breeds of dogs are named after, either the place they come from, or a specific person who bred them originally.
- Greeks have customarily named their babies after the father's parents. The French often use a child's middle name to pay homage to a set of grandparents, using both grandmother's first name for a girl and both grandfathers' names for a boy.

Similar expressions;

- To call after - to go by - to put a name to.

Pass around

Meaning; to offer something to each person in a group of people.

Examples;

➢ Take a copy for yourself and pass the rest around.

➢ Students at Concordia Language Villages held up and passed around an inflatable globe during International Day on Friday.

➢ Could you please pass around these bowls?" Jacob's mom asked him. As he handed a steaming bowl of soup to Barney, and one to Fred.

➢ Please pass around these copies of the agenda I prepared for you.

➢ I am going to pass around some homework. These pages are due Thursday. If you have any questions, feel free to ask.

➢ It was nearly midday and a pitiless sun was beating down. A rumor was passing around: "This was our destination, the camp of Ravensbru¨ck!" As our doors were pushed back, we saw extra guards, new ones, very severe- looking.

Similar expressions;

➢ To circulate - to pass on - to distribute - to circularize - to propagate - to broadcast - to spread - to diffuse - to disperse - to publicize - to air.

Pass away

Meaning; to die; to come to an end.

Examples;

- ➤ Adrien Arcand passed away in 1967, convinced that Canada would eventually embrace his views.
- ➤ I'd like to take you back to just before your loved one passed away. How did the two of you get along? Were you in close contact? Was their death expected?
- ➤ Lunch went well, and Sarah explained how her father had inherited the farm from his parents when they passed away, and how her father had then passed away and she came into the farm.
- ➤ My beloved sister Mary passed away of cancer in ISSU. She was only 5 years old. I still clearly remember Mum bringing something home for the younger children on her paydays at work.
- ➤ Our family had the greatest respect for Rachel Robinson, and it was natural to keep in touch with her after Jackie passed away.
- ➤ Everything is of a restricted duration, that everything arrives and passes away. Time, so it appears, is the restriction of duration through passing away.

Similar expressions;

- ➤ To depart - to rest in peace - to decease - to demise - to be taken/ to be dead - to be lost.

Pass out

Meaning; to become unconscious.

Examples;

➢ A half hour later, someone was on my floor talking about how he was in the hallway screaming again, but went back into his room and passed out.

➢ These physical causes may not be present now, but because sufferers have fainted in the past they may assume they will pass out again.

➢ I had passed out a few times, and as a result became more and more convinced that something was seriously going wrong.

➢ No sooner had I uttered a few words, I did in fact pass out. I came to with my head down and so heavy I felt like I couldn't lift it.

➢ He had no history and was on no medicines, and his story was that he had passed out twice that day. He said that before he passed out, he felt short of breath, got dizzy, then woke up feeling fine.

➢ Ken had passed out after he reached up and touched his ear, only to pull his hand away covered in blood.

Similar expressions;

➢ To lose consciousness - to **knock** someone **out** - to faint - to black out.

Pass on

Meaning;

1. to tell someone something that someone else has told you.
2. to give something to someone else.

Examples;

➤ The theological truth was the importance of passing on from generation to generation the truth of God.

➤ As channels, we exist not just to enjoy things but to pass them on. Our purpose is twofold: to flourish ourselves and to help others flourish.

➤ Any alteration of the DNA sequence is a mutation. Usually, an altered gene will be passed on to every cell that develops from it.

➤ He immediately began to hum the tune before me, from which, turning over the leaves of the note-book, he passed on to others, which he sang as he went along.

➤ The queen's mother, who in turn had passed the message on to the king, who had passed the message on to the groom, who had passed it on to the footman, and so on and so on.

➤ As we passed out (on) brochures at different plants late in the evenings, another of my colleagues Howard from the union would just happen to appear out of nowhere and eagerly join in.

Similar expressions;

1. To transfer - to convey - to send - to relate - to express.
2. To pass around/ out/ along - hand over - to distribute - to circulate - to spread out.

Pass by

Meaning;

1. to go past something or someone.
2. if something passes you by, you do not notice it.

Examples;

➤ Continue on Front Street, passing by more shops, the hospital, and a bank or two where you may exchange money.
➤ Be careful of time passing by quickly; avoid thinking of small problems and the daily obstacles and events that keep you away from your target.
➤ But one lady did say that the fact she didn't see anything didn't necessarily mean that a girl on a motorbike didn't pass by.
➤ Hundreds of people lined the main road to watch the president procession passing by.
➤ Through the café window I saw that same car passing by this street over and over again last night.
➤ Don't let another day pass by without checking out and evaluating the data.

Similar expressions;

1. To go by - to travel by - to move past - to go past.
2. To happen - to go by.

Pay back/ off

Meaning; to give someone the money that you borrowed from them.

Examples;

➢ How can we pay all these debts back. Things are going out of control and I'm totally hopeless.

➢ After a down payment of $4,000, the balance will be paid off in 48 equal monthly payments with the interest of 12% per year on the unpaid balance.

➢ You then pay off the debt a little at a time. Finally, when the debt is entirely paid off, you are allowed to execute the suspension.

➢ I was paying off my line of credit with the rent money and with as much of my income as I could.

➢ If you could have an interest-free loan, would you think that was a good idea? Not only interest-free, but you can pay it back for an extended period of time.

➢ So if I'm going to give you $100, first I'm going to ask myself, "What are the chances this guy's going to be able to pay me back?"

Similar expressions;

➢ To clear - to pay up - to repay - to settle up.

Pay for

Meaning;

1. to suffer because of something bad you have done;
2. to buy something; to give money to people for services.

Examples;

➢ A. "The comparison does not fit. The bills are based on the number of your appointments. We don't have a fixed fee for the whole duration of treatment."

➢ "I know that I will not pay for that appointment. Will you dismiss me because of that?"

➢ You will make mistakes; and you have the right because you are human to make those mistakes many times. At the end of the day, it is you who will pay for the mistakes you make.

➢ We have been assuring you that there is a lot of financial assistance available to help you pay for college.

➢ Still other citizens do not belong to any health plan but are able to pay for their care on a fee-for-service basis.

➢ They won't get away with it. They must pay for their misuse of power and taking advantage of people's need for urgent help.

➢ As far as I'm concerned, downloading music off the internet without paying for it is not a crime.

Similar expressions;

1. To pay a penalty - to be punished - to suffer the consequences - to pay the price - to get one's deserts - to take one's medicine.
2. To finance - to settle up for - to fund - to give payment to - to purchase.

Pay off   -   Come to fruition   -   Go places

Meaning; to yield go results; to succeed.

Examples;

➤ After years of striving and toiling, her persistence in regaining her rights as a mother finally paid off.

➤ Put a lot of efforts into building your skills up, and this will pay you off someday.

➤ Jane wanted to become a famous designer, but her dreams never came to fruition.

➤ The volunteers watched the villagers proudly as their plan came to fruition.

➤ As the fisherman saw his grandson working, he patted on his back and said; "I never thought you could perform such a perfect job! You'll go places my boy; just keep it up."

➤ What you think in the mental sphere will sooner or later find form in the realm of physical reality in one way or another. So, if you have a positive attitude, you will go places in life that you thought were never possible.

Similar expressions;

➤ To amount to something - to bear fruits - to go a long way - to make it - to make the grade - to fly high - to turn out well - to get results - to do the trick - to make good - to crack it.

Pick at

Meaning;

1. To be critical of or negative about someone or something.
2. to eat a small amount of food or without appetite.
3. to remove or pull something with one's fingertips.

Examples;

➢ Children usually pick at vegetables but when it comes to sweets they are just non-stoppable.

➢ The man fished two eggs out and put them in front of Red, who gingerly picked at them with a bent rusty fork

➢ Jenny seems to be on a diet. She just picked at her meal, forcing down a mouthful or two.

➢ The soldier was young, barely out of his teens and continually picked at a sore on his left cheek.

➢ Kathy picked at the pink line running the length of her forearm. She scratched at the thin scab covering an overlooked stitch, found a tiny knot and pulled it.

➢ The only problem was my co-workers couldn't stand me so they would pick at me here and there. When I was very young, Windom liked picking at me and making ugly faces.

Similar expressions;
1. To put down - to nag - to hassle - to provoke - to get at - to tease- to bully.
2. To nibble - to take small bites - to eat between meals - to eat like a bird - toy with - to peck at - to gnaw at - to snack on.
3. To pull out - to extract - to root out - to take out.

Pick up

Meaning;

1. To take something up with a hand; collect things.
2. To give a passenger a lift.
3. To learn or hear something.
4. To tidy or clean a room.
5. To increase.

Examples;

➤ One of the students leaned to the ground to pick up her wallet.
➤ I've got to pick up the books which I ordered or they will send them back.
➤ Could you do me a favor and pick up the kids from school today?
➤ The passengers put on their seat belts as the train began to pick up speed.
➤ What a mess! Can't you pick up the kitchen after you cook?
➤ The sterilized filter paper is gently set upon the Petri plate, where it absorbs moisture and picks up worms.
➤ I stood up to go. 'Thanks anyway'. I picked up my bag, then remembered something. 'I'm not sure you'd know about this'.
➤ He just picked it up all of a sudden. He had no formal lessons but he used to practice a lot.

Similar expressions;

1. To lift - to grasp - to gather - to raise - to uplift - to take up - to elevate.
2. To collect - to bring - to call for - to fetch.
3. To acquire skill in - to become competent in - to master - to digest.
4. To arrange - to straighten - to order - to organize.
5. To build up - to speed up - to step up.

Pile up

Meaning; to increase the amount of something a lot.

Examples;

> You're a dumb girl, Beth, playing with things you don't understand. You go to the dining hall and everything solidifies. Everything's gross. You're piling up cereals. piling up toast, and pasta aimlessly.

> The dark liquid inched up the sides of the jug and sent out a warm, earthy aroma that did its best to cancel out the snow piling up outside.

> (aH) is a parameter that relates the stress produced by dislocations piled up at an inclusion to the average strain.

> The lower bottoms are about twenty feet higher than the surface of low water; the trees on the beach are piled up by ice and drifted wood, to the height of four or five feet above the level of the ground.

> An idea struck him that perhaps these boxes had been piled up to conceal some passage leading out of the secret storeroom.

> We've let our emotions pile up to a dangerous level. And we amplify our feelings by bringing in a sense of entitlement.

Similar expressions;

> To accumulate - to add to - to stockpile - to make a bundle - to bring together - to compile - to heap together - to aggregate - to load up.

Point out

Meaning; to tell a fact; to make a person notice someone or something.

Examples;

➢ We'd better move on to the next step because we are running out of time and the flaws in the plan have already been pointed out.

➢ Researchers point out that dark green leafy vegetables are good sources of the vitamin.

➢ Anne pointed out that Mike's van had been in the car park all day and he was out of sight that day.

➢ What's great about the solution employee *is* that although they are also *pointing out* the problem, more importantly they are moving towards a solution.

➢ He *pointed out* that she *would* always be welcome *to* do some casual replacement teaching, as much as she wanted.

➢ Victor's teacher also tried to point out the probable causes for his misbehavior. When he knocked over the desk, the teacher would say, "I guess it's easier to get mad at the desk than to get mad at yourself because you can't do the math.

Similar expressions;

➢ To make clear - to put across - illustrate - to drive something home - to prove - to show - to explain - to indicate - to affirm - to state - to clear up - to make plain.

Pop/ Come up

Meaning; to suddenly appear or happen, often unexpectedly.

Examples;

➢ His shiny brown head *popped up* and he swept his wet hair out of his face. It was Mike. She would know those muscular arms anywhere. He was talking to someone out of her sight line.

➢ As I crossed over to this room, there were more green boxes that *popped up* on my computer screen than I could count.

➢ The process got more complex and we entered into a vicious cycle. As one problem appears to be resolved, two others pop up and the original *problem pops up* again, and so on.

➢ Even though he was off duty, he was still on call, in case something urgent came up.

➢ Mel went into Doc's every morning, the baby with her for the day. If something urgent came up, she could always take the baby over to Jack at the bar, or if Jack wasn't there, Mike was more than willing to babysit.

➢ Only an hour later it happened that the old landlord of the place came up for some instructions unexpectedly. His appearance freaked us out.

Similar expressions;

➢ To come into view - to come along - to turn up - to show up.

Pull away   -   Pull over

Meaning;
1. If a vehicle pulls away, it starts moving onto a road.
2. If a vehicle pulls over, it moves to the side of the road.

Examples;
➢ She threw her pack into the back of the truck before he could change his mind and climbed in using the wheel as a step. As the truck *pulled away*, she looked back for the first time.
➢ Miriam hated goodbyes. She hurriedly blew them a kiss as *the train pulled away* from the station. She held John tightly and settled back for the long trip.
➢ But before they could even get close to the train, a bell rang and the doors slammed shut. People left on the platform jumped back as *the train pulled away.*
➢ There is a true story about a man who was driving along the highway one night when he saw *a car pulled over* to the side of the road with a flat tire.
➢ He *pulled over* slightly to the right on the narrow road allowing the *car* some room to pass, but it stayed on his tail.
➢ Usually when I drive on this route, which is about four and a half to five hours, I can drive straight through without stopping for a bathroom break. Now, Coco is having a fit to go and I *have to pull over.*

Similar expressions;

1. To pull out - to pull off - to pull in - to depart - to leave - to hit the road - to move out - to move on - to get away.
2. To stop – to pull in – to draw up – to pull off the road – to park.

Put (something) up

Meaning;

1. to build something.
2. to fasten something to a wall or ceiling.
3. to increase the price or value of something.

Examples;

➤ We spent the weekend putting up a fence in the backyard.

➤ They are going to put up the prices of fuel.

➤ On the outer walls of the hut, which formed the other side of the passage, he had put up shelves, and there all kinds of tinned foods were stored. All was in such perfect order that one could put one's hand on what one wanted in the dark.

➤ It is likely that the 'royal visit' referred to was a state visit by the Thai royal family to London, during which EMI lent the Metropolitan Police two CCTV cameras to put up in Trafalgar Square.

➤ You don't pick me up, I will not hurt you. Helped the Mrs. put up new blinds in my sons room over the weekend.

➤ What is now called Mbeere District Hospital, as far as I know, and it is all there for everybody to see, is what was formerly Siakago Division Health Centre. Today, no extra buildings or other facilities have been put up.

Similar expressions;

1. To go up - to construct - to establish.
2. To raise - to erect - to make up - to install.
3. To build up - to move up - to come up - to pile up - to soar - to mount.

Put up with

Meaning; to accept unpleasant situation or experience; to endure or tolerate.

Examples;
➢ It was a long way back home; and I had to put up with a lot of daily complaining and nonsense from my travelling mates.
➢ Hanna was forced to bite the bullet and put up with her husband messing with her.
➢ I have been told that I should expect tough life conditions in the camp and that I have to put up with it.
➢ We want payback for the years that we have suffered, the years that we had *put up with* cockroaches and rats. We had *to put up with* snow, we had *to put up with* English, and we had *to put up with* racism.
➢ To tolerate something is *to put up with* it, which you only do if it's something you disapprove of, or don't like. If Kyle really doesn't mind being called a stinking Jew, then his letting it pass is not toleration.
➢ In order to do this, you have to define what you want, what you are willing *to put up with* and the lengths you're willing to go. Or, on the other hand, what you're not willing *to put up with* and the lengths you won't go.

Similar expressions;

➢ To tolerate - to accept - to stomach - to swallow - to bear - to stand - to take it - to lump it.

Put on

Meaning; to put clothes or shoes onto your body.

✓ **Opposite**: Take off.

Examples;

➢ Before you start, decide which *jacket* or *jackets* you would like to take off and/or *put* on. Try to focus on good breathing for thirty to forty seconds.

➢ John was out at the garden doing chores so there was no problem, but Elizabeth promptly asked Nina to *put on a dress* and prepare herself for a long trip.

➢ Fundamentally, people *put on their best* faces when they interview for a job; and often they do not tell the truth, the whole truth and nothing but the truth about their past.

➢ I met him right in front of Masters'. Jack was the essence of tactfulness and politeness, *took off his hat*, and accepted the invitation.

➢ Among *the* Orientals it has been customary to *take the shoes* from *the* feet to enter a house as *a* mark of respect and reverence as Americans *take off the* hat in similar circumstances.

➢ Muslims to this day always *take off their shoes* before they enter a mosque.

Similar expressions;

➢ To wear - to get dressed - to dress - to pull on - to have on - slip on - to throw on.

Put someone out

Meaning; to cause trouble or extra work for someone.

Examples;

- That meeting was a public one, and I did not intend going out; I told him that he knew very well that both he and his minister had been acting unlawfully in trying to put me out in front of the press.
- I don't mean to put you out or anything. I mean, if you're busy with something. I just feel like I could use a friend right now.
- Tanya told me that she was going to Georgia the next day and she wanted me to pick her up when she got back. I asked her in amazement, "You are trying to put me out and you want me to take you? Are you crazy?"
- "I am so sorry for putting you out." "I am never put out by you." Lainey blushed. "You helped me just by being there. I wish I could've done more."
- "Sorry for putting you out by showing up," he said with a grin, then spent dinner complaining about all the things Stephen's family had that he didn't have, or hadn't had growing up.
- I am sorry for putting you out, but you must understand that we do not tolerate nonsense in this family and your protection means everything to us.

Similar expressions;

- To bother - to trouble - to annoy - to make angry - to disturb - to irritate.

Put something out

Meaning;

1. to make something that is burning stop burning;
2. to produce information or something and make it available.

Examples;

➤ The fire was uncontrollable, one of those intense fires that no one was able to put out. Finally, in desperation, the oil well owner offered a three thousand reward to whomever could put out the fire.

➤ Quickly, she ran outside, and there was a fire just outside the window. She ran back into the house, filled a large bucket of water, and threw the water on the fire to put it out.

➤ An eight foot area of my roof was on fire. I grabbed my ladder and my buddy grabbed a hose. My wife ran in the house to call the fire department. We tried to put the fire out, but it was too big and already out of control.

➤ In a complex world, it's also not enough simply to put a product out there in a range of variations and through a variety of channels and hope for the best.

➤ When it got to the point where Capitol just absolutely refused to put out the album with that cover, he eventually gave in as they were running out of time.

➤ We put out a report this last year showing $10 billion worth of waste a year in the Justice Department. Here is a synopsis. Here is the report we put out.

Similar expressions;

1. To blow out - to extinguish - to douse - to stamp out.
2. To issue - to publish - to release - to bring out.

Put away

Meaning; to put something in the place where you usually keep it.

Examples;

- And the next time you make coffee, pour me a cup and put some bourbon in it and light me a cigarette and put it beside the cup. At last put it away in my letter case.
- How many times have you heard your mother or father complain about your clutter and say, "Please pick it up and put it away"?
- You have to pick up your goods somewhere, to load it in your car, unload it, and put it away.
- He, however, got the electric kettle out of a packing case and put it on the side. I put it away again.
- Pour over them cream and sugar, but no vinegar, etc. When dried hard, put them away for winter use. When you wish to cook them, put them to soak in cold water.
- There are two storage methods for clothes: one is to put them on hangers and hang from a rod and the other is to fold them and put them away in drawers.

Similar expressions;

- To put back - store away - to stow.

Put forward

Meaning; to state an idea or opinion, or to suggest a plan to be considered or discussed.

Examples;

- let me put forward my point of view in this regards." Everybody became silent. "In our world, we were undefeatable, uncatchable and invincible.
- Many biotech companies put forward their claims that GMO are substantial scientific breakthrough which provide feed to the world, to decrease poverty especially in developing countries and to save the environment.
- Mr. Covell put forward a suggestion that it would be advantageous if a person with more business experience was asked to join the committee.
- Party members and cadres had put forward many valuable suggestions, but in the later stage of the movement, these suggestions were regarded as standing on shaky grounds in the socialist road.
- Try to put forward solutions and recommendations that are not only technically sound but also politically acceptable and administratively feasible.
- The report put forward a plan to restore the environment, economy, and public health of residents.

Similar expressions;

- To recommend - to advance - to nominate - to propose - to submit

Put someone down

Meaning;

1. to criticize.
2. to write someone's name on a list for doing something.

Examples;

➢ I don't know if the sighted go through some of the obstacles that the blind have to go through. People tend to overlook me and put me down.

➢ It was so terrifying to see her waiting for me to pass by her, to listen to her insults, putting me down like a school yard bully.

➢ I have had plenty of experience with people who like to put you down and make you feel small. This happened a great deal in my family who seemed to think that if they put you down, it made them okay.

➢ I put his name down in a book at that time, thinking it strange that any one should pay men to come to Harrisburg.

➢ Sir John said he had promised him his freedom three or four years before that, and desired his name should be put down in the list.

➢ In the tea break Marjorie reminded us that we should put our names down on a list if we wanted to join the Christmas lunch party at the end of term.

Similar expressions;

1. To dress down - to belittle - to humiliate - to abuse - to bad-mouth - to offend - to reproach - to tear down - to slander.
2. To jot down - to record - to transcribe - to take down.

Put off

Meaning; To delay something or arrange to do it at a later time.

- **Opposite**; bring forward.

Examples;

- ➤ I think he feared he might lose me to someone else, if you can believe it," she added with a sad smile. "I've put it off, but I fear I can put it off no longer."
- ➤ Can you put it off a couple of days, I really need a day of rest and a couple of hot showers, oh yeah, and some sleep.
- ➤ I finally took a train from New York to Boston for the doctor's appointment I had been putting off for month.
- ➤ I'm afraid that the idea to bring the date of the exhibition forward isn't workable after we have distributed the invitation cards.
- ➤ The officials are in a hurry to put an end to the crisis and they will bring the discussion session forward as a result.
- ➤ We're overjoyed that you've brought the date of the appointment forward because we are pressed for time.

Similar expressions;

- ➤ To defer - to delay - to hold off - to postpone - to put back.

Rat/ Report on   -   A Whistleblower

Meaning; to inform on or against someone.

Examples;

➢ Under this test, an employee-whistleblower would not have to prove that his or her allegations of misconduct were in fact correct.

➢ It had become evident that state whistleblowing statutes in the United States, passed to protect whistleblowers and encourage reporting, were not very effective.

➢ It was through a whistleblower that the activities at Abu Ghraib came to light.

➢ When she asked the name of my school, I felt like I was a traitor, ratting on Mrs. G. by admitting I hadn't been given anything to teach.

➢ And another thing, if either one of you gossips ever decide to rat on us to the police or your parents or anyone else, well, me and my cousins here will have to come and finish this little job.

➢ He asserts that misconduct among lawyers remains largely unreported because lawyers are reluctant to report on each other.

Similar expressions;

➢ To blow the whistle on - to squeal - to tell tales on - to peach on - to sell out - to stab in the back - to report on - to be disloyal to.

Rip-off - Rip someone off

Meaning; something that costs far too much money.

Examples;

➢ The biggest rip-off of all when travel agents take your money and give you nothing in return.

➢ It seemed like a rip-off when compared to the old pension plan in which the employer carried all of the risks and expense.

➢ Most times, however, companies interested in ripping off success use a cosmetic approach but sacrifice on choice of material and manufacturing quality.

➢ Everywhere you look there are more and more scams to rip people off. I go on E-Bay, I get ripped off, the internet, I get ripped off, watch television and see the so called home businesses and you get ripped off.

➢ They're called Stradivarius." "All right then. Give me five bucks for it." "Five bucks for a Stradivarius?" I said. "That's a rip-off.

➢ If you choose to do business with less-recognized vendors, they might not be directly trying to rip you off, but odds are something isn't right.

Similar expressions;

➢ To defraud - to swindle - to overcharge.

Rough up

Meaning; to attack someone physically. To scrape or rub something.

Examples;

➢ "Wait, straight up, I'm being serious now," Avery changed his tone and said. "Okay, creeps, jerks, hoodlums, guys that have no problem roughing up you, me, or your mom."

➢ Quarter bosses could overstep their bounds (for example, by roughing up the wrong person or banishing someone from the town without the mill superintendent's permission).

➢ The strongman continued to show his contempt for democracy by roughing up the political opposition and making mass political arrests.

➢ She is kind of a parent who roughs you up to make you tough for the real world.

➢ Overland shipping is cheapest, but usually takes a few months to get there and items may get roughed up a bit on the way.

➢ If I do get irritated I feel my energy level drops. Oftentimes, I get roughed up over something that is almost pointless. Like when my brother Neil misplaces again his door key and cannot find it.

Similar expressions;

➢ To beat up - to hit - to knock around - to mistreat - to abuse - to handle harshly.

Run away

Meaning; to escape from a place, person, or situation.

Examples;

➢ The owner used to tell us that if the police ever come, run away before they can catch you, so I knew that when the police come, I'll be taken away from there.

➢ The FYSB study concluded that familial substance abuse had an adverse effect on juvenile behavioral problems such as running away from home

➢ Their father and mother, seeing them busy at their work, got away from them insensibly, and ran away from them all at once.

➢ I'm going to run away from here as soon as I feel better. I'm going to find Thomas's wife and tell her what you did. "I'm not putting the dress on," I tell her. "If you don't, I'll get Henry up here, and we'll strip you and put it on you ourselves."

➢ Unable to contemplate the wolf as a wolf and to consider whether running away is the best course of action, the sheep simply automatically runs away.

➢ Another good question of a type which is seldom asked is: Why do antelopes run away from lions instead of hitting back?

Similar expressions;

➢ To flee - to get away - to run off - to run for it, take flight - to make off - to take off - to take to one's heels - to make a break for it - to beat a (hasty) retreat - to clear out - to clear off - to get out of.

Run out of   -   Run short of

Meaning; to use almost all of something and there is not much left.

Examples;

➢ But if you are always running short on office supplies, about the legal structure of running short of patience, and running short of time to deal with paperwork, then having the wrong legal structure for your business will spell the disaster.

➢ Both crews were on short allowance. The provisions were running short, and the summer season was closing.

➢ When the people ran short of food during the holy battles, or the food of their families in Al-Madina ran short, they would collect all their remaining food in one sheet.

➢ I am convinced that, under present conditions and the way water is being managed, we will run out of water long before we run out of fuel.

➢ Tired of your mobile phone or laptop battery running out of power at inopportune times? Well, portable fuel cells just might be the solution.

➢ For many of us the first thing we do when we get home is make sure our phone gets recharged. The warning that comes up on your phone when it's running out of battery power: "Alert! You're running below 20% percent!" Unfortunately we don't have some indicator to alerts us when our bodies run out of energy.

Similar expressions;

➢ To be used up - to dry up - to be exhausted - to peter out - to fail - to exhaust.

Run over

Meaning; to hit someone or something with a vehicle and drive over them.

Examples;

- ➢ A couple were on their way to a luncheon at a restaurant in an area mall. As they were driving on a curvy road, they ran over a cat.
- ➢ He pointed toward her car, which had a flat back tire. "I must have run over something." "I don't think you ran over something, the tires are worn out."
- ➢ Marin gasped, and looked to her left and saw someone running away just as the train came barreling down the tracks. Screaming, she came out of the vision just before the train ran over the woman.
- ➢ The German divisional commander had been injured when a lorry ran over his leg while he slept in the open.
- ➢ You can imagine how surprised I was when I nearly ran over one on my way in. I knew the robots interacted with one another, but I didn't expect to be greeted by one.
- ➢ I tried calling someone on my phone but my battery was dead. I kept looking in the rearview mirror so often I almost ran over an old lady struggling with her aluminum walker on the curb.

Similar expressions;

- ➢ To crash - to smash into - to strike - to bump into - to knock - to lay flat.

Run/ Spread through

Meaning; to pervade; to be present in every part.

Examples;

- She locked the door behind him and leaned against it, puzzling over his strange behavior. A cold shiver ran through her whole body.
- It was mentioned there might be a third, and then no harm could happen to the suitors, unless corruption ran through the whole office.
- Those, and other similar remarks spread through the crowd until the whispers were so many in number that they created quite a din.
- It was Gregory, who was determined to stamp out the growing hysteria before it ran riot throughout the whole city.
- You could follow the tracks there because the tracks ran through the whole river valley.
- The fame of my services and talents ran through the whole Country. Every good man respected me. I was invited to visit people in all parts of the provinces.

Similar expressions;

- To extend - to fill - to go through.

Rush to (do) something

Meaning; to do something quickly and enthusiastically.

Examples;

➢ I seem to have spent my whole life rushing to get somewhere. Rushing to school, rushing to work, rushing to get home to get ready for a date I was already late for.

➢ Chances are, you will find people rushing from one place to another, busying themselves silly. Caught in a mad rush, we are always rushing from point A to point B, rushing to finish one chore after another.

➢ After the evening at the Opry, they rushed to a concert in Atlanta, Georgia. Then, in a pouring rain, they packed up all the instruments and their personal belongings, rushed to the airport, and flew to Houston.

➢ The firemen rushed to the building with hoses, axes, and pick poles. Laura looked in horror and screamed for Jim. The medics rushed to Jim and put him on a stretcher with an oxygen mask.

➢ Set your alarm and a back-up alarm so you do not oversleep and then have to rush to get to the testing center on time.

➢ Heading for her sixth period class, she felt someone rush to catch up with her and begin to walk with her.

Similar expressions;

➢ To hurry - to dash - to race - to bound - to fly - to speed - to race the clock - to bustle - to hasten - to whisk.

Save up (for)

Meaning; to keep money so that you can buy something with it in the future.

Examples;

➢ Suppose you want a new computer or bike. But other things cost more, so you need to save up for those things. That's why many people save their money in a bank account. You will not forget to save your money if it is in the bank.

➢ It is recommended that you save up at least six months of your current income before you start relying on your business for your primary income.

➢ It would take me over 26 years to save up for the house, and that's forgetting that the house would probably go up in value.

➢ It was her one doll that she owned as a toy playmate which concerned the little girl. All she wanted was a better looking outfit that would make her look pretty. Mom and dad saved up for this as most of us would take it for granted.

➢ While it may seem difficult to reprioritize your needs, you can set up a savings account attached to specific goals, such as saving up for your baby.

➢ A miser begins by saving up for a rainy day, and ends by saving up for the rainy days of his heirs.

Similar expressions;

➢ To lay aside - to save for a rainy day - to store away - to reserve - to pile up - to scrimp - to amass - to economize - to spare - to be thrifty - scrimp and save.

Set foot in/on

Meaning; to go to or enter a place.

Examples;

➢ I have never given him a reason to question my loyalty. But Connor's death will encourage Henry to intervene. You will disappear after it is done and never set foot in Ireland again.

➢ Twenty years ago when he left Stone Creek, he'd promised himself never to set foot in this place again.

➢ When a cook got drunk one evening at the Union Square house and CVS went to see what the fuss was about, it marked the first time he had set foot in his own kitchen.

➢ At the age of thirty-eight, Neil Armstrong had become the first person to set foot on the moon.

➢ My son, if sinners entice you, do not give in to them; do not go along with them, do not set foot on their paths.

➢ This happened several years before Howard and I married, and as far as I know before Ruth's death, he never set foot on the farm for any reason.

Similar expressions;

➢ To show up - to pass in - to land - to cross threshold - to come.

Set off

Meaning;

1. to start a journey.
2. to make something start working.

Examples;

➤ When the lights turned to green, the lorry slowly set off with me tucked in behind him.

➤ I reloaded and set off after it down the stony incline, and succeeded in sending a bullet through its shoulder, which felled it to the ground.

➤ The tricks of criminals, such as cutting wires, turning off the power, or jumping wires before forcing a window, will set off the alarm.

➤ The 1994 movie Natural Born Killers set off a chain reaction of violence and bloodshed that reached across the United States.

➤ I was just about to set off for work when the mail dropped through our letterbox. Judy, our little black and tan dog, had a nasty habit of attacking whatever came through the letterbox.

➤ While a very few have been explorers who aimed for charting new territory and new routes to far-off lands, most have simply set off on a journey from their home port to a distant destination.

Similar expressions;

1. To set out - to set forth - to begin one's journey - to hit the road - to start out - to depart - to leave - to embark.
2. To trigger - to start off - to bring about - to account for - to effect - to launch.

Set up

Meaning;

1. to start a business, company or organization.
2. to organize or plan something; to build or prepare something.

Examples;

➢ This action list looks at the advantages and disadvantages of companies, and describes how to set up a business as a company. It also discusses other relevant issues including administrative and accounting responsibilities.

➢ In the 1990s I went on a photo safari holiday and was awakened to the possibilities of wildlife photography. I submitted these images to a photo agency and later set up my own agency.

➢ How you arrange your groups is up to you. Base your organization principle on whatever makes sense to you and fits the groups you set up.

➢ Set up a schedule to provide meals for the family. Perhaps you can babysit some of the other children in the family during this time and set up a schedule for others within the group to serve in this way.

➢ Police have set up several roadblocks and checkpoints on the road to the city.

➢ James helped me set up the table, and then he cleared it on his own. I don't know how to return his favors.

Similar expressions;

1. To establish - to launch - to open - to put up - to initiate - to originate - to install - to compose - to create - to construct.
2. To make ready - to design - to schedule - to scheme - to harmonize - to direct - to set stage - to shape up - to prepare.

Settle down

Meaning;

1. to start living in a place where you intend to stay with a partner
2. to start to feel happy and confident with a new situation.

Examples;

➢ It will only be possible to discern the implications for price formation once the new regime has settled down and its actual costs can be observed.

➢ When the market has settled down with the equilibrium price, buyers and sellers will all settle down.

➢ Finding that one special person you are willing to settle down with, to share the rest of your life with seems like it will never happen at times.

➢ This was the city where I proposed to settle down after returning from abroad. I was deliberating as to where I should settle down for the rest of my life, some friends advised me to settle down in the United States.

➢ Some of family values can be willingness to settle down, willingness for taking responsibilities and willingness for heading a household.

➢ When are you going to settle down, Harry? You can't play around forever.' 'Don't try and ruin my fun. There's no point even thinking about settling down until I find somewhere to settle.'

Similar expressions;

1. To get married - to become wise - to grow up - to reason.
2. To calm down - to relax - to progress - to develop - be accustomed to.

Shake up

Meaning;

1. To make someone feel surprised, shocked or upset.
2. To move something up and down or from side to side.

Examples;

➤ If the students were allowed to slip into the middle of another nonproductive year, it would be difficult to shake them up and ignite a fire under them.

➤ We want the film to shake us up, to thrill us, to show us wonders, to frighten us, to make us wince, to give us chills, to build tension in us and release it, and to be unsettlingly familiar as well as original.

➤ If we can understand our inner selves, we will become content, and any situation we face does not shake us up, does not make us unhappy, and we experience less sorrow, depression, anger, and frustration.

➤ I'm not saying I want you to hurt her, but couldn't we make something happen just to shake her up? So she would think twice about what she does.

➤ Momma told Daddy to shake the bottle up so that the candy doesn't settle to the bottom of the bottle.

➤ Put the cap on the bottle and shake it up, so the food coloring mixes through the bottle.

Similar expressions;

1. To shock - to turn upside down - to cause revolution - to overturn - to disturb - to bother - to ruin.
2. To move - to jiggle - to goggle - to wave from side to side.

Show off

Meaning; to display one's abilities or achievements boastfully.

Examples;

- Once in a while all of us do it. Even adults like to show off their cars or impress people with how much they know. Nature is filled with creatures that like to do things to get attention.
- The norm, the desirable, in masculine societies is that one wants to shine, to show one's success. Success is communicated, shared, and displayed because it is natural to show off.
- The Strip was where all the Latino's went once a month to show off their cars and listen to their music. The bosses come out to show that they are a boss - smoke and drink, the ladies get a chance to show off their new outfits and jewels.
- Well, I'm sure I thought he was showing off and rubbing my nose in the fact that he could do something better than I could.
- One Saturday night when my parents were away, I drove my car to the teen club, and was showing off in front of my friends.
- To spend money with this motive of showing off is to waste it. The evil of such waste can ruin people's future on the long run.

Similar expressions;

- To boast - to brag - to crow - to trumpet - to blow one's trumpet - to swagger around - to put on airs - to strike a pose - to draw attention to one's self.

Slack off

Meaning; to be lazy or inefficient; not to work hard.

Examples;

➤ Don't imagine that once you've got your bonus, you feel good, and you can slack off. The major type of corruption is slackness.

➤ Those who don't do their job after having earned some money are slacking off. As a company employee, should I work hard or slack off? What if the people around me are slacking off and getting away with it?

➤ Those employees who slack off in the final weeks should expect less than positive recommendations. Commit yourself to leaving your job with honor and dignity. Remember that the last impression is the one that will always be remembered.

➤ JACK, "It's not an excuse for you to slack off because you assume I'll bail you out." DANE, "I'm not slacking off. I wanted to tell you, I've kind of had a hard time focusing."

➤ That's just it—if you can't let your employees work from home out of fear, they'll slack off without your supervision, you're a babysitter, not a manager. Remote work is very likely the least of your problems.

➤ Just remember when you're tempted to slack off that you can have worry-free fun after the work is done. Reward yourself.

Similar expressions;

➤ To ease off - to idle - to lay back - to slow down - to tapper - to dwindle.

Sort out

Meaning;

1. To organize; to set in order.
2. To deal with something successfully.

Examples;

➢ This guide is useful for sorting out home visits, sorting out the reasons to try to improve behavior, and sorting out guarantees to students and staff.

➢ The problem seemed to have been there forever and it was something that had never been sorted out.

➢ Look! I realize that the pair of you have issues that you need to sort out but throwing stools through the window and upsetting all of the other guests in the park is not going to sort it out for you. Neither of the couple said anything.

➢ When Brian came on the scene as a manager, we realized what a manager meant because Brian then took the bookings, sorted out the money, got us a few quid, sorted out the tax, sorted out the publicity. We'd never had that before.

➢ Tom's in charge of the music, and trying to make sure that everyone gets a prize. Mum's helping to organize things while I sort out the soft drinks for afterwards.

➢ One just gets lost if one gets thrown into the heap, so if you spend your life trying to sort out each heap, you just get confused, and you will come to the conclusion that it's hopeless.

Similar expressions;

1. To arrange - to classify - to line up - to group - to adjust - to regulate.
2. To fix - to iron out - to deal with - to straighten out - to repair - to handle - to solve - to manage - to settle - to troubleshoot.

Stand by

Meaning;

1. To take any action to stop something bad happening.
2. To support or remain loyal.

Examples;

➢ I will not stand by or remain passive as I watch my men die when I had the chance to save them.

➢ But what I won't do, I won't stand by and watch you make the same mistakes I made.

➢ Dress rehearsal had gone reasonably well, though not brilliantly, but the drama teacher standing by to help told Sarah that was a good sign.

➢ Having said that, there were the faithful few who stood by us at all times, especially Uncle Kalu, Aunty Louise, and Aunty Kate. For better or for worse, that's how we married.

➢ In war, soldiers fighting for a just cause ought to stand by their post when attacked.

➢ Never hesitate or think of backing off. I will stand by you and look after you to the last gasp.

Similar expressions;

1. To make no move - to sit by - to stand aside.
2. To remain/be loyal to - stand up for - to be supportive of - to back - to back up - to uphold - to defend - to stick up for.

Step down

Meaning: to leave an important job.

Examples;

➤ He stepped down as the manager of the Italian team.
➤ He stated that he believed Marcos would have to step down and that he was losing power rapidly.
➤ He came and said he had accepted the call to step down and to take up the new position thrust on him.
➤ Letting them know if they do not resolve the problem they will be asked to step down (especially if the problem involves a sin issue).
➤ But then he called and said Vitteli had agreed to step down; it seemed like it was all going to work out.
➤ The US Air Force had already launched the first two waves of aircraft (a total of 60 C-130s) loaded with US Army Airborne troops and equipment rigged for airdrop when the military government agreed to step down.

Similar expressions;

➤ To resign - to stand down - to give up one's post/job - to bow out - to retire - to abdicate - to quit

Step in

Meaning: to become involved in a difficult situation in order to help.

Examples;

➢ A Japanese bank stepped in to provide financial help.

➢ Fate stepped in and saved the day for I met you on that faithful day Oh what a sight to behold an angel of light shining so bright.

➢ When they were baffled about how to feed and care for the multitudes who often followed him hither and yon, he stepped in and saved the day.

➢ Both sons had rejected him, moved out as soon as they could, didn't stay in touch, not until irony stepped in to keep them together.

➢ "He won't escape you good citizens this time," came the reply, "unless his angels step in and pull him through the roof." Realizing she must stay out of sight, Louisa pressed close to a big maple tree.

➢ Things were getting ugly when a guy stepped in and rescued my brother and me from the mob. Turns out he was a Yankees fan himself. We thanked him profusely and he just laughed and said, "You are cool kids.

Similar expressions;

➢ To intervene - to intercede - to become/get involved - to act - to take action - to take measures - to take a hand - to mediate - to arbitrate - to intermediate.

Step on it /the gas   -   Speed up

Meaning; to be or drive faster.

- ✓ **Opposite**; Slow down.

Examples;

- ➤ Three men were waving along the road, but Steven stepped on the gas and went ahead.
- ➤ I didn't know which direction I was going through. However, I decided not to ask and stepped on the gas.
- ➤ The road was rough and the car started to slow down. I stepped on the gas pedal and started to ask God not to let me break down in that dreadful place.
- ➤ John had to speed up as we were getting late for the event. The car surged forward as George stepped on the gas. Everyone went mad and asked him to slow down.
- ➤ Jenny was stepping on the gas with all her strength. She nearly hit the wall but the car suddenly broke down.
- ➤ Bangkok was the worst place for traffic I ever saw; no lights, you just step on the gas and race five hundred other cars to the crossing. The main rule of Asian driving seems to be: never use the brake, just lean on the horn.
- ➤ This drug may have the effect of speeding up your heart rate.

Similar expressions;

- ➤ To hurry up - to get a move on - to go faster - to pick up speed.

Start over/ afresh

Meaning; to begin to do something again, sometimes in a different way.

Examples;

➤ We decided to abandon the first draft of the report and start over.
➤ The agreement allows old expectations to be forgotten and everyone can start afresh.
➤ This is full of errors - I'm going to have to start over.
➤ If you make a mistake, you have to start over.
➤ Can I make these few corrections or do I have to start over?
➤ I'm looking forward to starting afresh in a new town with a new job.
➤ A new house gives you the chance to start afresh.

Similar expressions;

➤ To restart - to relaunch - to make a new start/beginning - to return to the beginning - to start from scratch/zero - to make a fresh start.

String along with   -   Stick together

Meaning; to go along with someone, to accompany or follow.

Examples;

➢ You'll be hearing from me. You take my advice - string along with me. I know this business inside and out. You forget about starving for Art's sake. That won't keep you alive five minutes. You've got to be ruthless.

➢ I'm not refusing anything, yet. I'm just saying I like the law. I'll string along, within reason. You certainly have a right to clear this room.

➢ Are you a master manipulator who can string along several partners at the same time? You must think I'm a fool, someone you can string along until you get a better offer.

➢ We kids are going to stop the bullies and show all of our classmates we don't have to be scared to come to school if we stick together and stick up for ourselves! Together, we can do it and we will!

➢ Will the family stick together during these trying times today? Or will the problems in our lives take us all separate ways? Do we still find joy in sharing, like our elders did before?

➢ The business men of the town continued to hold meetings and pass resolutions to stick together. They argued that all they had to do to save the town was to stick together.

Similar expressions;

➢ To go along - to join up with - to join in - to take up with - to stick to.

Sum up   -   In a nutshell

Meaning; to summarize; to give a summary of. In the fewest possible words.

Examples;

➢ Speak up in a strong tone of voice without asking for permission or making apologies. Before you leave the room, briefly sum up the discussion, describing what each person has agreed to do.

➢ That memory of riding on the bus from field to field pretty much sums up the life we led. In a lot of ways it's a world that time forgot, essentially unchanged over decades.

➢ If I wanted to sum up my life and sum up for people what they can do in life, I would sum it up in six words: "Man becomes what he thinks about."

➢ George; "Why are you back this fast? What went wrong?"

➢ Ian; "In a nutshell, everything."

➢ Nobody could make progress in transforming lead into gold. Take my word for it my dear. It's all lies in a nutshell.

➢ In few minutes I learned her life story in a nutshell. She and her son had that much in common. I learned she couldn't possibly survive without a feline companion, that she loved to read but only mysteries.

Similar expressions;

➢ To outline - to recap - to review - to put in a nutshell - to give the gist - to give an abstract.

Take after

Meaning; to resemble or behave as an older member of one's family.

Examples;

➤ There were the distractions of the city as they made the rounds of the museums. She thought Frank an exceptionally handsome man, and Martha took after him, if she took after anyone.

➤ Yes, some of us took after Dad and some after Mom. Me and Zella and Josie a little bit took after your granddaddy. He was tall, had a high forehead, and a Roman nose. Like mine.

➤ She wondered for a moment what their children would look like? Whether they would take after her, and be gypsies, or whether they would take after Gavril, and be cursed? The thought made her go weak at the knees.

➤ The three got together at the hotel. They make a wonderful team. We are very proud of them, especially Gary. His looks take after his deceased Uncle Joey.

➤ "My! What handsome lads! You take after your father, Alfonso. Same good looks!" Alfonso blushed. She grabbed Ronnie's cheeks in both hands.

➤ You've grown quite a lot since I was last here, and you take after your mother, not that you wouldn't look good taking after your father.

Similar expressions;

➤ To look like - to be like - to be similar to - to bear a resemblance to - to have the look of - to remind one of - to make one think of - to cause one to remember - to call up - to be the spitting image of.

Take away - A takeaway

Meaning:

1. to buy food in a restaurant and eat it somewhere else
2. to learn something from an experience or activity.

Examples;

➤ If there is one thing that people should take away from Black Tuesday, it is that we need regulators.
➤ What I took away from his talk is that going to university is definitely worth it.
➤ On Monday evenings we were always too tired to cook so we ordered takeaways.
➤ In New York you can get a huge range of takeaway food cheaper than cooking at home.
➤ I am simply trying to point out that life needs balance. The takeaway here is that some of life's toughest, most painful experiences can also have the best results in the long run.
➤ There were lots of takeaways I could use. It helped me do my work better. The session was interactive where I could try out what was taught and got feedback on how I did. There was warmth and humor and I learned a lot from the other participants.

Similar expressions;

➤ Food: to take out - to carry away - to carry out - to grab and go.
➤ Ideas: to conclude - to get the gist - to deduce - to summarize - to figure.

Take (someone) for (someone – something)

Meaning; to wrongly believe something about someone.

Examples;

➤ Why don't you call him now? What do you take me for? A simpleton.

➤ You've indeed gone too far. Haven't you offended me enough? What do you take me for?

➤ They're taking us for cowards. Right? We're just waiting for the right time to show them who we really are.

➤ Excuse me, Charles! I couldn't recognize you. You've changed a lot since we last met. I took you for a stranger.

➤ What's the matter Bob? Your clothes are so ragged. I almost took you for a beggar.

➤ What do you mean, Sir? What do you take me for? Do you think I am so ignorant of the world, as to imagine that I am to prescribe to a gentleman?

Similar expressions;

➤ To misjudge - to miscalculate.

Take it out on

Meaning; to mistreat other people or things because of your anger or frustration.

Examples;

- I think bullies are hurting inside and they don't know how to express themselves very well and so they take it out on others.
- After years of this, it occurred to me that I had bad days at work, too, and I did take it out on everyone else.
- Now when I do school visits, I often share my adopted philosophy on dealing with hard times: Don't take your anger out on yourself (through drugs or alcohol or whatever), don't take it out on other people (by being negative or aggressive).
- Even worse, in many cases, the man won't be able to take it out on his mother, so he'll take it out on his wife.
- It was because there was so little to do in Welch; maybe it was because life there was hard and it put all the miners in bad moods. They came home and took it out on their wives, who took it out on their kids.
- I knew he was going through a lot right now. When he was home, he sometimes took his frustrations out on his family and some other times on me.

Similar expressions;

- To vent - to give off - to unleash - to bother - to harass - to pick at - to provoke.

Take off

Meaning;

1. (a plane); to start flying.
2. to become more successful.
3. to remove clothing.

Examples;

➢ I took off my purple sneakers and put them under my bed. Mom wouldn't notice anything weird about me going around the house in socks.

➢ Take off your shoes and put them neatly in the appropriate place. Inside, walk clockwise around the perimeter.

➢ As mentioned before, time between take off and arrivals which involves taxi, passenger drop off, visual controls, is the minimum required time for the plane to take off again.

➢ Take care of yourself on your way back. What time does your flight take off? What is the departure time of your flight?

➢ Often, such personal savings along with a small unsecured bank loan can be enough to get the business off the ground. Waiting for your business to take off can be discouraging, but try to remain optimistic.

➢ I would like to appeal to the Ministry to ensure that the sum of money left is taken to Homa Bay immediately so that the co-operative project takes off.

Similar expressions;

1. To leave the ground - to take to the air - to take wing - to lift off.
2. To do well - to progress - to become popular - to flourish - to grow.
3. To strip - to remove.

Take over

Meaning; to start doing something that someone else was doing; to take control.

Examples;

➢ After the attacker knows the sequence numbers, he has to take one of the parties offline so he can take over the session.

➢ It is absolutely imperative to express your feelings because bitterness will try to take over.

➢ Well, the last thing that I remember is waking up on some island, and once I regained my strength, I swam back to the city, and I saw the Dark Panther and his thugs trying to take over the city.

➢ She will be in charge of the group as I am right now. One of the ladies will be sleeping, and when she awakes she will take this position and I will assume a guard position. That lady will relieve another and take over her assignment.

➢ Father thought he would take over this newspaper and make it into one of the most competitive publications in the state of Maine.

➢ You know what, you guys have been at it for a while now and you need a break, so I'll take over.

Similar expressions;

➢ To substitute - to be in the place of - to fill in for - to back up - to cover for - to take another's place - to take charge of - to handle - to take the lead.

Take place

Meaning; to occur; to happen.

Examples;

➤ The best transactions are taking place thanks to the advanced marketing strategies that has been introduced recently.

➤ The marriage ceremonies took place in various locations. In the early days, most marriages did not take place in a church. Many took place in the home of the bride, or the bride's parents.

➤ The century deserves particular attention not just because it immediately preceded the colonial period but also because of the significant events and revolutionary changes which took place within it.

➤ On the way, while passing through another piece of woodland, Alison somehow managed to break free and a struggle took place.

➤ Following a long period of avoiding the material elements of design and concentrating purely on the event and performing space, the latest project of

➤ taking place is a public art project for Homerton Hospital in London.

➤ The Conference will take place in Brazil on 20-22 June 2012 to mark the 20th anniversary of the 1992 United Nations.

Similar expressions;

➤ To come about - to befall - to come to pass - to transpire.

Take part in

Meaning; to join in an activity; to be involved.

Examples;

➢ People who are able to take part in cooperation are more willing to do so. In the end, it is the extent of interactivity which determines this degree of cooperation.

➢ Take part in the team building exercise. Take part in a discussion about why you want to get involved in the campaign. Take part in the what I want to achieve exercise.

➢ Violence inflicted in wartime influences people in a drastic way because the whole community takes part in war.

➢ This takes place in the form of a worldwide video conference in which some 1,850 members of management from over 50 countries take part.

➢ We studied patients taking part in an ambulatory rehabilitation program or those who were at least interested in them.

➢ Indeed, many Muslims will also take part in these celebrations on the basis that they are an international event which concerns all the inhabitants of the earth.

Similar expressions;

➢ To participate - to join in - to get involved - to enter - to share in - to play a part - to play a role - to be a participant - to partake - to contribute.

Take in

Meaning;

1. To accommodate.
2. To make clothing narrower.
3. To understand.

Examples;

➤ There are a lot of families in this town who take in foreign students.
➤ The viewers made a complete mess at the end of the show. I found it impossible to take in what was going on.
➤ Unfortunately, the hotel is full today. We can't take in any more guests.
➤ These instructions are really mixed-up; I can't take them in on my own. I would be grateful if someone points them out.
➤ I was pressed for time and I wasn't able to go to the tailor, so I asked mum to take the jeans in for me.
➤ Why don't you take this dress in. It's too loose - it doesn't fit you like this.

Similar expressions;

1. To house - to provide shelter for - to put up - to shelter.
2. To cut - to trim - to snip - to even up - to shape.
3. To make out - to comprehend - to grasp - to crack - to figure out.

Take on

Meaning;

1. To employ someone;
2. To begin to have a new form, appearance or character.
3. To fight or compete against.
4. To accept work or responsibility

Examples;

➤ We're not taking on any new staff at the moment.
➤ Our website is taking on a new look.
➤ This evening Manchester United take on Barcelona.
➤ We'll be taking on two new members of staff.
➤ I might take you on at tennis sometime.
➤ Her voice took on a tone of authority.
➤ Don't take on more than you can handle.
➤ Why did you take on this assignment if you're so busy?

Similar expressions;

1. To hire - to recruit - take into employment - to enroll - to appoint.
2. To begin - to arise - to originate - to pick up.
3. To challenge - to defy - to face.
4. To carry responsibility for - to take charge of - allow for.

Take up

Meaning;

1. Start doing something new.
2. to occupy or use space/time.

Examples;

➤ This fridge doesn't fit well in our kitchen. It will take up too much space.

➤ An examination of the Myriad Ways guys splay their legs on subway trains taking up too much space, seemingly oblivious to other riders desperate for a seat.

➤ If you have any large games installed, consider removing them first, because they usually take up substantial amounts of hard disk space.

➤ Basketball was the most common sport in the Japanese Americans communities. Nevertheless, they took up football fervently during the first four decades of the twentieth century.

➤ You can go back to school, embark on a new career or a new business, or take up a new hobby.

➤ A few years later he left his employer to take up a sailing opportunity he couldn't combine with his work.

Similar expressions;

1. To start on - to make a start - to get into - to enter on.
2. To fill - to stuff - to pack - to overload - to pad.

Talk back

Meaning; To talk back to is to respond in an impolite way to an adult.

Examples;

➢ Chinese children are always taught never to talk back to their parents.

➢ But now many of them can stand up in front of the gate and talk back to the managing director.

➢ You must be out of your mind today - how could you talk back to your boss like that?

➢ In those days verbal punishment weren't banned and if we talked back to the teacher, we got two strokes on the palm.

➢ Nothing seemed to irritate white southerners more than when blacks talked back to them with even the slightest hint of insolence. Nevertheless, slave resistance sometimes took the form of verbal protest against ill treatment.

➢ It bothered me, but I had nobody to talk to. After all, we had been warned, within an inch of our lives, that we never talked about anything in the family outside of the family. We were never allowed to talk back, so I went to my room and sobbed.

Similar expressions;

➢ To answer back - to answer defiantly - to be impertinent - to answer impertinently - to be cheeky - to be rude - to contradict - to argue with - to disagree with.

Tear up

Meaning; to destroy something such as a cloth or paper into small pieces.

Examples;

➢ Not only did Lucky tear up the papers, but Toby learned to tear them up, too. When I was home, I took them outside.

➢ So then I just told her to grow up, and to leave, that I was too old for babies. They said if I didn't tear up that contract and stay away from Heather, I wouldn't live to see my next birthday.

➢ When he gets back to New York he can tear up the temporary passport, or tear up the old one and get a new one.

➢ But when they got there, those mob crowds had got in there, in the house, and tore up all of their groceries and poured it in the middle of the floor.

➢ The intruders tore up his civilian ID card and wrecked his home. His wife was manhandled and his sister was mercilessly kicked.

➢ Anything that wasn't expressly candy or dessert was good for you, whether it was battered, fried, or whatever cut of meat. After two bowls, my gums were torn up and hurting, but I wouldn't stop until the bowl was empty.

Similar expressions;

➢ To ruin - to devastate - to rip apart - to ravage - to shatter - to smash into pieces - to crush - to knock something out - to trash.

Think over

Meaning; to think carefully and at length before taking a decision.

Examples;

➢ Beth, you think over a fight, you think over a move to another apartment, you think over a vacation, you don't think over a baby!

➢ I still need to think over it. He too felt the same thing and wanted me to take enough time to think over it as it's a very important decision. We then bid goodbye to each other and left.

➢ When you think over and over about what you don't want, you end up getting what you pay the most attention to; the thing you don't want! When you think over and over about what makes you happy, you bring happiness into your life.

➢ You could think it's wishful thinking on her part. Or you could think it's a constructive stance worth considering. It all depends on you. But don't make any rush decisions. You should take your time thinking it over.

➢ An answer such as: 'let me think it over, let me sleep on it,' would have been a sign of real weakening or hesitation.

➢ You really are terrific. We can really go places together, places that two people can't go on their own. I really believe that. You don't have to answer me right away. Take some time to think it over.

Similar expressions;

➢ Think twice before doing something - to consider - to turn over in one's mind - to digest - to think deeply.

Throw up

Meaning;

1. to vomit
2. to produce or build new things

Examples;

- ➤ I felt so frazzled, so frustrated, so ready to throw up only for more than 30 minutes of the that frustrating meeting.
- ➤ Throwing up after every meal means you don't get enough nutrition from food and therefore no energy.
- ➤ I got up and ran into the bathroom, I threw up in the tub I couldn't make it to the toilet I turned the shower on and threw up some more. As I lay down I threw up again. I threw up on the sidewalk.
- ➤ Higher aggregate incomes will throw up newer opportunities and ideas of new products and services resulting in the increase of high-tech and luxury products, entertainment, vehicles, durables, travel, etc.
- ➤ Even when one has learned to smoothly inhabit a way of life and a set of practices that comprise it, these practices and this way of life will continue to throw up challenges.
- ➤ The deaths of mothers, the wickedness of stepmothers, the complicity of their brides, the parents who abandon their children: all these harsh features of fairy tales throw up one storytelling challenge after another.

Similar expressions;

1. To be sick - to regurgitate - to be nauseous - to blow girts - to discharge.
2. To make up - to construct - to invent - to set up - to result in.

Try (something) on

Meaning; to put on a piece of clothing to see whether it fits; to test or examine something on someone or something.

Examples;

➢ Bill tried on almost every running shoe in the store before he found the pair he wanted.

➢ The advantage of shopping in a store is that you can try on clothes before buying them.

➢ "Is there a bathroom on board where I can try it on?" "Yeah, but it's small. You won't be able to move around in there," the woman said, returning Nicki's credit card with a receipt. "Better just to try it here."

➢ Deirdre had just finished the dress she was working on and she held it up for Mary to inspect. The four girls begged her to try it on but Mary seemed doubtful.

➢ You probably would not want to try this method on people with whom you are not familiar. Nor would you want to try it on someone who may not follow your advice or good will.

➢ In hot summers, this field was generally very much burnt up previous to the application of Salt. I was first induced to try it on arable land, on a field of wheat early in the Spring.

Similar expressions;

➢ To test - to experiment - to give a try - to check out - to sample - to put into practice - to inspect - to have a fitting.

Try (something) out

Meaning: to use something to discover if it works or if you like it.

Examples;

➢ Can you imagine how it feels to be a block on the top of the building you made? Let's try it out.

➢ It may seem like a tempting idea compared to the drudgery of your nine to five job, but do you really have enough commitment to see it through? One way to find out is to try it out for yourself. If you want to open a restaurant, get a job as a waiter.

➢ Children who came hoping to try out the latest Street-fighter games nearly ended up in street fights themselves.

➢ Don't forget to try out the equipment before setting up the experiment.

➢ We tried out the new song on a couple of friends, but they didn't like it.

➢ Dylan's latest record is a conscious attempt to break away from his old image and try out a new style.

Similar expressions;

➢ To test - to prove - to try - to examine - to essay - to evaluate - to pass judgment - to judge - to experiment - to audition - to perform.

Turn out

Meaning; to be discovered to be something; to develop in a particular way.

Examples;

➢ As it turned out, the car broke down halfway to the town and they had to stay there until midnight.

➢ I started out cycling as a hobbyist, but then turned out to be a professional athlete.

➢ It turned out that the company which we are dealing right now with was the same overseas company that supplied us with engines ten years ago.

➢ To our disappointment, it turned out that our partners were discussing offers with the bank behind our backs.

➢ To our surprise, the trainees turned out to be internet junkies and technology addicts.

➢ If it turns out that my best wasn't good enough, at least I won't look back and say that I was afraid to try; failure makes me even work harder.

Similar expressions;

➢ To prove to be - to become apparent - to be disclosed - to be revealed - to result - to end up - to appear.

Turn down

Meaning; to refuse an offer or request.

Examples;

- ➢ A narrow-minded woman like Lucy will certainly turn down any constructive suggestion.
- ➢ To his surprise, the bank turned his request down, saying they didn't think it would be a safe loan.
- ➢ You communicate best when there is rapport between you and the seller. The reason you want to build rapport is to get the seller to like you. If the seller likes you, it will be harder to turn down your offer.
- ➢ If I have to turn down a job, I say "I'm sorry I can't fit that into my schedule right now;" it would be irresponsible of me to try when my schedule's so full.
- ➢ Whenever an invitation arrives you search for a reason to turn it down; travel plans are cut because you are too busy at the office.
- ➢ Victor had even thought about asking Fantasy to marry him, but he knew she would turn him down.

Similar expressions;

- ➢ To reject - to decline - to rebuff - to decline - to dismiss.

Turn on/ off

Meaning;

1. turn on: make something start working.
2. turn off: make something stop working.

Examples;

➤ He opened the door and stepped in. He then closed and locked the door, turned on his PC, and emptied his pockets.

➤ As he boarded the seven forty two to Hull that morning he had not the slightest idea that his journey home would not be the normal mundane trip. Arriving in the office he sat at his desk and turned on his PC.

➤ One, the man, went to the TV mounted near the ceiling in the near corner of the room and turned it on then adjusted the settings. The old man could not focus on the TV to see what was playing.

➤ Of course, these sensors will automatically turn off the luminaires a few minutes after motion is no longer detected.

➤ I walked across the threshold to turn the light on, and I ran into somebody. It took my breath away. I said, 'Excuse me,' but there was nobody here but me. It was very strange, but I felt like I ran into somebody. I turned off the lights and came back.

➤ The device is turned on by applying a short pulse across the gate and cathode. Once the device turns on, the gate loses its control to turn off the device.

Similar expressions;

➤ (turn on): to switch on - to activate - to energize - to stimulate - to prompt.

(turn off): to switch off - to shut down - to close - to end - to finish.

Turn/Show up

Meaning; to arrive; to make an appearance.

Examples;

➢ If you fail to turn up for the interview on time, you have to try your luck at a later time.

➢ Some of the women eventually turned up alive, some turned up dead from drug overdoses.

➢ The wagon driver turned right and began circumventing the steepest part of the hill, eventually turning up Sixth Avenue where the slope was not so steep.

➢ I'll admit that Sandra Thornton apparently dropped out of sight for a couple of years but she eventually turned up again.

➢ The people who want a sofa bed really want a sofa bed, but they will never show up in your store unless you tell them you have that sofa.

➢ What if no one showed up when the community theater presented its plays? What if no one showed up for the school or community band concert? What if no one showed up for a student's piano recital?

Similar examples;

➢ To show up - to appear - to get to - to pop up - to be present - to turn out.

Warm up

Meaning;
1. To prepare for something.
2. To make machine etc ready.
3. To become interesting/busy.

Examples;

➢ The players are already on the field warming up.

➢ stretching exercises to warm up your calf muscles.

➢ In cold weather it takes longer for the car to warm up.

➢ The party was only just starting to warm up as I left.

➢ If you don't warm up before exercising, you risk injuring yourself.

➢ I might just warm up the leftovers from yesterday's meal in the microwave.

➢ He allowed the engine to tick over for 5 minutes to make it warm up gradually.

➢ She says a massage will help loosen you up and get the blood flowing normally and warm up those aching muscles.

Similar expressions;

1. To exercise - to loosen up - to work out - to stretch - to get ready.
2. To activate - to start up.
3. To improve - to look up - to catch up - to get better.

Watch out (for)

Meaning; to tell someone to be careful because they are in danger.

Examples;

➤ During the day we would explore the surrounding terrain always with a warning to watch out for wild animals and the dreaded snakes.

➤ The dog wrinkled his brow and cocked his head to one side. 'I'm warning you,' Mr Jenkinshaw sighed, 'you'd better watch out for that dog'.

➤ Watch out when they try to avoid their own responsibility by projecting it as someone else's liability.

➤ Almost everyone is happy when things go their way, but watch out when things don't go their way.

➤ The warning message said watch out. He wants things from you. He will steal things from you. Watch your guns. Watch your jewelry.

➤ Hey watch out! You almost hit us. Are you drunk or something? The other day you were arrested because of your reckless driving.

Similar expressions;

➤ To watch one's step - to be careful - to beware - to take care - to take heed - to look out - to mind - to notice.

Wear off/ away

Meaning; to lose effectiveness or intensity.

Examples;

➤ When newness of something wears off, then the priority of taking care of them and loving them begins to fade.

➤ Worried of its quick wear off? Then, stop doing the below given things. There are few things that you do will wear off your nail polish like the washing your hands with chemicals or doing the washing up without putting on gloves.

➤ Smoking creates a temporary wall between you and your stress and the feelings of stress return as soon as the effect wears off.

➤ Western students, over there, were quickly charmed and impressed by his teaching. But being temperamental, the excitement wears off in no more than a few days.

➤ The pain is so intense that I can feel my face distorting, so still believing it to be a passing wind, I cannot even lie down, and in the early hours of the morning the painkillers wear off and I'm in great pain again.

➤ After a standard workday in front of a computer, I return home to realize that the PVD coating is wearing away on the watchband.

Similar expressions;

➤ To fade - to melt away - to lose strength - to fizzle out - to weaken - to lessen - to subside - to grow faint - to evaporate - to vanish - to disappear - to ebb.

Wear out

Meaning;

1. To make someone extremely tired.
2. To make something old or damaged so that it cannot be used anymore.

Examples;

➤ Stepping on the brakes unnecessarily and constantly will cause the tires to wear out right away and prematurely.

➤ When you're mad at someone else, that emotion can linger, festering in your mind until it's a daily aggravation that weighs you down and wears you out.

➤ When we say something's worn out, all kinds of things could be wrong. A pair of shoes might wear out because you've gradually scraped the soles into holes through friction.

➤ If you go for an early morning walk on dewy grass you will soon notice that going barefoot makes you feel really good, generating new strength when you have been feeling tired and worn out. It is like recharging one's batteries, so to speak.

➤ A life without purpose is empty and often why people are so stressed, sad, and depressed. You feel worn out by all you have to do and the busyness of life with 24/7 technologies.

➤ For some men, the crotch of their trousers wears out too quickly. Heat and friction wears away even the most expensive wool fabrics.

Similar expressions;

1. To burn out - to exhaust - to tire - to drain - to wear down.
2. To destroy - to exhaust - to spoil - to waste - to wash up.

Weigh down

Meaning; to burden someone or something.

Examples;

➢ Those heavy hardbound textbooks weighed down the children the same way as worry and fear weighed down our spirits heavily.

➢ All these delays and interruptions are weighing us down and causing us to lose trust in our abilities in hitting our targets.

➢ Eventually, all the insights, conclusions, principles, and history begin to weigh us down as we carry them everywhere.

➢ There is a theory that it's unwise to put tasks on your to-do list that you will want to do six months or a year down the road. It weighs down your thoughts, preventing you from feeling like you are making progress.

➢ An anxious heart weighs a man down, but a kind word cheers him up. A righteous man is cautious in friendship.

➢ We are overweight in thought, which is weighing down our mind; overweight in stuff, weighing down our homes; and overweight in emotion, putting a heavy burden on our soul.

Similar expressions;

➢ To get down - to hold down - to oppress - to distress - to dismay - overload - to overburden - to trouble - to weigh upon - to worry - to sadden - to press.

Win over

Meaning;

1. To succeed in persuading someone to agree with you.
2. To overcome or defeat.

Examples;

➤ But as the days passed into weeks and the weeks turned into months, Ronda was won over by this man who treated Emily so warmly.

➤ Walking out of fear means you have overcome it, you have the victory over it. If you have won over fear, you can now say, "I have walked out of it."

➤ If you are making a sales pitch to a group of people, you can learn who you have won over, who is on the fence, or who is in opposition by monitoring the nonverbal gestures displayed by your audience.

➤ We can learn greatly from Tamar, of her wittiness, that finally won over her continued disappointment.

➤ He won over the elite by protecting their economic and judicial interests; he won over the urban poor by proposing public work projects, a ceiling on grain prices, and military reforms.

➤ With his dragon and his armies, he's won over most of the lords in the land. Those he can't frighten, he buys with silver. And now, he's got the due date of that Contract coming up!

Similar expressions;

1. To win over - to talk round - to bring round - to reason with.
2. To prevail over - to triumph over - to gain a victory against - to wipe - the floor with - to overpower - to make mincemeat of - to destroy.

Wind down

Meaning; to make something gradually end; to gradually relax.

Examples;

➢ "I had to wind down a practice and turn things over to other partners," she explained. "I was in the middle of a debt structuring for a co-op and a refinance and some FERC proceedings and a merger case."

➢ Anyway, as everything started to really wind down, the whole group came flowing into this one interior room and started getting themselves comfortable on the floor.

➢ When the discussion started winding down, T.K. suggested a paper ballot vote. When all of the votes were checked a few minutes later, the vote was unanimous to bring both Jeff and Rose into the group.

➢ The Second Law of Thermodynamics states, in essence, that without continual inputs of energy, all systems wind down.

➢ We needed some quiet after the long day to wind down. All the announcements about tomorrow could have been handled later in our rooms.

➢ The dance was winding down except for the guitar and the harmonica playing and Bursey Harper.

Similar expressions;

➢ (people) to ease off - to cool down - to rest - to take it easy - to chill out.

➢ (things) to come to an end - to taper off - to slow down - to diminish - to decline - to slacken off - to phase out - to close down.

Wipe out

Meaning;

1. To destroy something or someone completely.
2. To remove a substance, usually liquid, with a cloth.
3. To make someone tired.

Examples;

➢ I guess seeing Mia yesterday just wiped me out. I can't believe I slept so long.

➢ Fish and frogs don't mix well, as fish eat tadpoles, and the fish started wiping out frogs from lake after lake.

➢ 'Expiation' means a recompense of wrong acts, and 'atonement' means wiping out one's sins.

➢ With our greater visibility, I became increasingly afraid of waking up the sleeping giants, the big packaged food companies. If they had begun to sell specialty coffee early on, they could have wiped us out.

➢ I was slowing down and getting out of breath, but it was still fun. As time went on, the fatigue lasted longer. Just walking up the stairs, or to my car, wiped me out.

➢ As the class trooped out, I wiped the board out and wrote mosquito in large letters. The next class came in. "Where do I sit, sir?" asked a girl. "Oh, anywhere you like" I replied.

Similar expressions;

1. To defeat - to knock off - to shoot down - to overcome - to outshine.
2. To get rid of - to black out - to eliminate - to erase - to clean.
3. To exhaust - to wear out - to burn out to tire - to wear down.

Work on

Meaning; to spend time producing or improving something.

Examples;

- ➢ I could not pinpoint who was working on which samples. Often, two people would find out they were working on the same problem. We were experiencing data overload, and we were consequently overwhelmed.
- ➢ She trained as an architect at Chulalon University and joined the Thai government's National Housing in 1977, initially working on slum upgrading.
- ➢ Building common ground with people who are not like you is one of the most important skills you can develop in today's multicultural world. As you work on developing this skill, you will find that people are getting more and more understanding.
- ➢ I worked on my adviser's program of research but applied his research on new faculty members to research on the experiences of graduate students.
- ➢ To focus on getting things done and the sense of accomplishment will help you be more productive. Find a friend or co-worker who is also working on this and talk about your downfalls, achievements, and discoveries.
- ➢ I have worked on seven cartoons, and each production crew was different from the next, as the studios I have worked for were completely different.

Similar expressions;

- ➢ To work at - to build up - to perfect - to practice - to develop - to hone.

Work out

Meaning;

1. to understand someone or something; **(make out)**
2. to solve a problem by doing a calculation.
3. to do physical exercise.
4. to have a good result.

Examples;

➢ We had to change plans every now and then because most things didn't work out the way we had expected.
➢ To keep in shape is a matter of persistence and consistency. You must follow a balanced diet and work out a lot.
➢ Although three engineers were assigned to help us out, it took us four weeks to work out the value of last year's exports.
➢ Unless you optimize the existing premises of the place, chances are the new plan will not work out.
➢ Who on earth does this paper belong to? How can I grade it; I can't even work out a word of it.
➢ Sally's new roommate is a wired girl – she is hopeless at working her out.
➢ Nothing works out if we keep taking things for granted. It's time we took responsibility and put an end to this farce.

Similar expressions;

1. To comprehend - to make out - to get the idea - to be in tune with.
2. To calculate - to make out - to solve - to assess - to multiply.
3. To burn off - to firm up - to do exercises - to train.
4. To succeed - to turn out well - to get results - to do the trick - to be do the business - to be effective - to pay off - to come off.

CPSIA information can be obtained
at www.ICGtesting.com
Printed in the USA
LVHW091557090519
617264LV00004B/807/P

9 781729 105955